Credibility Without Rules?
Monetary Frameworks in the Post–Bretton Woods Era

Carlo Cottarelli and Curzio Giannini

INTERNATIONAL MONETARY FUND
Washington DC
December 1997

Composition: Alicia Etchebarne-Bourdin

Cataloging-in-Publication Data

Cottarelli, Carlo
    Credibility without rules? : monetary frameworks in the Post–Bretton Woods era / Carlo Cottarelli and Curzio Giannini—Washington, DC : International Monetary Fund, 1997.

        p.   cm. — (Occasional paper , ISSN 0251-6365 / International Monetary Fund ; 154)

    ISBN 1-55775-644-9

    1. Monetary policy—History—20th century. 2. Monetary policy—Developing countries. 3. Banks and banking, Central. 4. International Monetary Fund. I. Giannini, Curzio. II. Title. III. Series: Occasional Paper (International Monetary Fund) ; no. 154.
HG230.3.C65   1997

Price: US$18.00
(US$15.00 to full-time faculty members and
students at universities and colleges)

Please send orders to:
International Monetary Fund, Publication Services
700 19th Street, N.W., Washington, D.C. 20431, U.S.A.
Tel.: (202) 623-7430   Telefax: (202) 623-7201
E-mail: publications@imf.org
Internet: http://www.imf.org

recycled paper

Contents

Appendix

Figures

Section

The following symbols have been used throughout this paper:

. . . to indicate that data are not available;

— to indicate that the figure is zero or less than half the final digit shown, or that the item does not exist;

– between years or months (e.g., 1994–95 or January–June) to indicate the years or months covered, including the beginning and ending years or months;

/ between years (e.g., 1994/95) to indicate a crop or fiscal (financial) year.

"Billion" means a thousand million.

Minor discrepancies between constituent figures and totals are due to rounding.

The term "country," as used in this paper, does not in all cases refer to a territorial entity that is a state as understood by international law and practice; the term also covers some territorial entities that are not states, but for which statistical data are maintained and provided internationally on a separate and independent basis.

Preface

This paper was prepared by Carlo Cottarelli, Division Chief in the European I Department of the IMF, and by Curzio Giannini, Deputy Director in the Research Department of the Banca d'Italia. Most of it was prepared during 1995, when Carlo Cottarelli was a member of the Monetary and Exchange Affairs Department of the IMF. A first draft of the paper was presented at the XI World Congress of the International Economic Association, held in Tunis, on December 18–22, 1995. The paper greatly benefited from comments and suggestions from William E. Alexander, Lorenzo Bini Smaghi, Manuel Guitián, Eduart Hochreiter, Arto Kovanen, Francesco Lippi, Gian Maria Milesi-Ferretti, Carlo Monticelli, Chrys Ryan, Massimo Roccas, and Daniele Terlizzese. David Driscoll and Martha Bonilla of the External Relations Department edited the manuscript for publication and coordinated production. The views expressed in the paper, as well as any errors, are the sole responsibility of the authors and should not be construed to be those of the Executive Directors of the IMF or any other members of the IMF or the Banca d'Italia staff.

Grau, teurer Freund, ist alle Theorie,
Und grün des Lebens goldner Baum.
(Grey, dear Friend, is all theory, and
green is life's golden tree.)

—*Goethe, Faust*

The whole point of the Doomsday
Machine is lost if you keep it a secret!
Why didn't you tell the world, eh?
—*Stanley Kubrick, "Dr. Strangelove"*

I Introduction

During the last quarter of a century, the theory and practice of monetary policy have undergone momentous changes. At the practical level, a world in which monetary policies had to be managed, at least in principle, within the code of conduct of the Bretton Woods system was replaced 25 years ago by a world where the rules of the game—the monetary framework, in current economic jargon—are markedly different across countries and bear little resemblance to those prevailing during the Bretton Woods era.

The evolution of monetary theory has been equally dramatic. At the end of the 1960s, mainstream macroeconomics regarded monetary management (and more generally economic management) mostly as a "game against nature" in which the optimal setting of monetary instruments could be determined by solving the economy's econometric model after imputing desired policy targets. There had been debate between supporters of discretion-based policies and of rule-based policies (à la Friedman) on the degree of knowledge of the model's parameters, and hence on the feasibility of activist policies. But the concept that monetary discretion could, in principle, be optimally used was virtually undisputed. Since the mid-1970s, this view has been gradually abandoned: in a change that bears some similarities with the "quantum mechanics" revolution in physics during the 1920s, the "state of nature" (certain key parameters of the economic model reflecting the response to policy actions) stopped being regarded as independent from the actions of the observer (the policymaker). Of course, economic models are still formulated in

terms of fixed coefficients, but these mostly describe the agents' (including the authorities') utilities functions rather than fixed responses to policy instruments. Since then, monetary policy has been described primarily as a game between the policymaker and one or more representative agents (trade unions, enterprises, and, sometimes, the "government" as distinct from the monetary policymaker). Concepts and theories borrowed from politics and warfare theory—such as credibility and deterrence—became increasingly common.

This paper provides a chronicle of the evolution of the theory and practice of monetary policy during the last 25 years. It focuses on monetary frameworks, that is, on the announced basic principles and institutional rules guiding the execution of monetary policy. There have been previous attempts to discuss the evolution of monetary frameworks, but only in individual countries or in a limited number of countries, typically industrial countries (Bernanke and Mishkin (1992)). The first novelty of this paper lies in the breadth of the data base. The paper monitors the evolution of the monetary framework in 100 countries or country unions between 1970 and 1994 (a total of 2,500 observations, see Appendix). The sample includes almost all independent nations in existence during that period, with the exclusion of centrally planned economies and countries disrupted by wars or civil strife.

A second novelty is methodological. Most empirical studies of monetary policy take both society's preferences and the overall institutional environment as given. This assumption clearly will not do when one wants to investigate the long-run factors leading to a change of monetary framework. Indeed, the fundamental function performed by a monetary framework is to facilitate monetary exchange while preserving the trust in price stability or, more precisely, in the predictability of the future price level. How well a given monetary framework is going to perform this task will depend on prevailing perceptions and preferences, the structural features of the economy, and the nature and performance of a whole set of other institutions. All these factors, of course, change over time.

The paper argues that during the last 25 years, monetary practice in most countries has increasingly been characterized by the attempt to achieve credibility of purpose while expanding the freedom of monetary authorities in controlling policy instruments. Thus, the world has gradually moved toward monetary frameworks in which, through appropriate institutional devices, a better trade-off between credibility of goals and flexibility of instruments could be achieved. This attempt, discernible in most countries surveyed in the paper, has taken different forms, depending on the countries' economic, institutional, and cultural specificities.

The structure of the paper is as follows. Section II highlights the driving forces behind the changes in monetary frameworks in the post–Bretton Woods period and points at the increasing relevance in monetary theory of the credibility issue in the context of fiat standards. It also notes the emerging concept of "delegation" as a way to improve the credibility-flexibility trade-off. Against this background, Section III describes the evolution of monetary frameworks in the sample countries, highlighting the gradual shift away from rule-based frameworks toward more discretion-based policies. Section IV contrasts the decline of rule-based frameworks with the spreading of frameworks in which credibility is achieved through alternative institutional devices, centered on delegation and increased transparency. In industrial countries, these devices have taken the form of increased central bank independence and inflation targeting, while in developing countries, delegation to the International Monetary Fund has become increasingly common. The role of reputational equilibria is also discussed. Finally, this section focuses on the interrelation between monetary institutions and the development of an ethos of price stability, without which these institutions would not be viable in the long run. Section V looks more closely at some features of the rule-based frameworks, and in particular at the relative role of monetary and exchange rate-based frameworks, discussing the future of foreign exchange anchors in a world of increased capital mobility. Section VI summarizes the main findings of the paper.[1]

---

[1]The paper does not try to assess to what extent macroeconomic performance is affected by the monetary framework, as recently done with reference to the exchange rate regime by Ghosh and others (1995).

II Degenerating Fiat Standard and Credibility

Institutions do not evolve in a piecemeal fashion for a number of reasons. First of all, adapting an institutional framework involves collective action at several levels (North (1990)). Second, and perhaps more significant, adaptation must be preceded by widespread recognition not only of the need to reform the existing setup, but also of the set of feasible reform options. Such a choice is fraught with difficulties, especially since often no theoretical benchmark exists against which to evaluate the welfare properties of alternative reform schemes. This happens because the need for institutional reform is typically predicated on imperfections or forms of market incompleteness that prevent the attainment of Pareto optimality. As argued by Demsetz (1967), in such circumstances, it would be incorrect to gauge the relative attractiveness of alternative reform schemes by contrasting them with the unattainable optimum. When dealing with institutions, the proof of the pudding is inescapably in the eating.

All this helps to explain why the adaptation of most real-world institutions seems to follow a recurrent pattern, hinging on three phases: a period of "incubation," during which pressures mount, without leading, however, to an explicit demand for reform; a "crisis" phase, during which there emerge new phenomena, not easily explained on the basis of existing institutions or conceptual models; and, finally, a phase in which the need for adaptation is increasingly recognized, with the emerging consensus tending, however, to favor parsimonious reform schemes, that is, schemes that retain as much as possible of the extant setup.

The adaptation of the monetary framework is no exception to this by now well-recognized pattern.[2] This section shows that the wave of alterations in the monetary frameworks that followed the demise of the Bretton Woods system conforms to this pattern. The wave was set in motion by the emergence of a previously unknown macrophenomenon—stagflation. In the lively debate that ensued, proposals for far-fetched reform eventually gave way to less ambitious schemes, which carried the promise of ridding the fiat standard of its inflationary bias without sacrificing its superior flexibility with respect to other standards.

Degenerating Fiat Standard

After the switch from the gold standard to the fiat standard, which was for all practical purposes completed in the postwar years with the nationalization of most of the world's central banks, matters related to the monetary standard practically disappeared from both theory and policy discussions. In spite of Irving Fisher's famous warning against the perils of fiat money, inflation remained for more than two decades at about 2 percent in industrial countries, hardly an unbearable rate. At the same time, the world economy developed at an unprecedented pace (Flood and Mussa (1994)).

The international monetary system created at Bretton Woods, which exerted a disciplining influence on national economic policies, deserves part of the credit for this remarkable performance. But other forces were at play. The first two decades after the war, for instance, were marked by widespread skepticism about the effectiveness of monetary policy. As a consequence, the monetary lever was hardly used: rather than actively stimulating the economy, which was rapidly growing anyway, the authorities preferred to concentrate on stabilizing long-term interest rates (Guitián (1994b)). Thus, in the context of rapidly growing economies, authorities did not need to avail themselves fully of the flexibility the fiat standard allowed, which lay at the root of Irving Fisher's misgivings.

Things started to go wrong when, toward the mid-1960s, growth rates slowed considerably throughout the industrial world. In the context of lower growth, the fixity of exchange rates mandated de facto, if not de jure, by the Bretton Woods institutions, started to be felt as a constraint on domestic economic policies. As a result, among other things, of monetary policies turning increasingly activist, inflation started acceler-

---

[2]On the long-run evolution of monetary institutions, see Eggertsson (1990) and Giannini (1995).

ating in most industrial countries in 1963–64 (Bordo (1993)).

The history of international monetary relations in the second half of the 1960s is by and large the story of the attempt to fix what had by then become a faltering monetary framework without confronting squarely the fundamental problem, namely its incompatibility with the mounting demand for policy activism. One often-overlooked feature of the period marked by the fall of the Bretton Woods' exchange rate system is the conflict that developed between central bankers and politicians over the appropriate conduct of monetary policy. One after another, in many industrial countries, central bank governors were either abruptly dismissed or duly subdued (Giannini (1994)).

This is not the place to review in detail the enormous literature on the causes of the inflation upsurge of the 1970s. For our purposes, suffice it to note that available evidence suggests "that any reasonably plausible explanation . . . will include substantial components of ignorance and error . . . and Government irresponsibility" (Smith (1992)). Both factors, however, would have been harmless without popular emphasis on the need to combat unemployment at the expense of the inflationary consequence of monetary activism. As former Federal Reserve Board Chairman Arthur Burns lamented in his self-defense against the allegation of monetary laxity, the search for monetary flexibility reflected deeper and for the while uncheckable trends in society (Burns (1987)).[3]

Thus, by the mid-1970s the fiat standard, finally freed from the constraints set by Bretton Woods' multilateral peg system, had become a degenerating monetary framework: the passive monetary stance of the first decades after its establishment had been replaced by an activist stance, spurred by popular concern that the era of fast growth was in danger.

Debate on Monetary Standard

Support for activist monetary policies started to falter when inflation began to be associated with rapidly mounting unemployment (Lindberg and Maier (1985), Bruno and Sachs (1985)). Stagflation

seems to have played the same contributing role as it did during the Great Depression in the 1930s or during the recurring banking crises in the late nineteenth century: that is, it signaled unequivocally both the degeneration of the existing monetary framework and the inadequacy of existing theories to confront the challenge. The impact stagflation made at the time is captured by the U.S. Council of Economic Advisers' Report for 1974, which, after trying to make sense of the inflation upsurge in the context of mounting unemployment, somberly concluded that "there is no simple explanation for this price behavior, which was the most extraordinary in almost a generation and which confounded the Council and most other economists alike." That something had gone wrong by the mid-1970s was unquestionable; what precisely it was, and how it was to be put to right, remained to be established. It should therefore come as no surprise that in the second half of the 1970s, the debate on the "monetary standard," which had lain dormant, with rare and short-lived awakenings, for at least four decades, came back with renewed strength.

There was a novelty, though. Previous bouts of the debate had hinged on the relative merits (and drawbacks) of rule-based and discretion-based monetary frameworks.[4] The outcome of the debate had appeared to be clear cut. If one believed that the effects of monetary policy, at least in the short run, were highly unpredictable (Milton Friedman's famous "long and variable lags"), then activist (discretionary) policies were of little use. If one believed that policymakers had sufficient knowledge of a few key parameters of the economic system, then discretion, guided by all available information and backed by optimal control techniques, was preferable (B. Friedman (1975)). The latter view had appeared more attractive to most economists, partly because of the new econometric techniques developed during the 1950s and 1960s.

This view was shattered by a few influential papers showing that a policymaker unbounded by rules had an incentive to "cheat" the private sector in order to either keep unemployment below its natural rate or increase seigniorage by raising inflation. As argued by Kydland and Prescott (1977) and later shown more forcefully by Barro and Gordon (1983a), since rational agents discount the incentive of the policymaker to engineer surprise inflation, they will adjust their behavior accordingly. As a result, the economy will be subject to an inflation bias: inflation will be above target, but to no avail for the unemployment rate.

---

[3]Smith (1992), for instance, quotes survey data for Britain showing that in 1972, when forced to choose between higher unemployment and higher inflation, most income groups opted for the latter. As to the United States, Gallup survey data on "the Nation's Most Important Problem" (reported in Fischer (1996)) provide a similar indication: during the first half of the 1960s, the ratio between those who regarded unemployment as the most serious problem with respect to those who regarded inflation as the most important problem reached a historical peak. However, the absolute percentage of the first group remains altogether quite small.

---

[4]See, for example, the collection of papers edited by Yeager (1962).

Kydland and Prescott (1977) and Barro and Gordon (1983a) saw their demonstration of the inflationary bias of discretionary policy as making the case for a monetary rule, along Friedman lines (Fischer (1995a)). Others reached even more radical conclusions, for instance, that the inflation bias could not be effectively used without taking control of the money supply out of the government's hands. As a result, at the turn of the 1980s, a vast number of far-reaching proposals for monetary reform appeared in the literature. Hayek (1978) and White (1984), for example, advocated the repeal of the state monopoly in the supply of base money. Other scholars, sufficiently influential to win the establishment of a U.S. Senate Commission to investigate the matter, argued in favor of a return to the gold standard.[5] Greenfield and Yeager (1993), Hall (1983), and Fama (1980) suggested instead possible schemes for separating the unit of account from the means of payment.[6] Finally, M. Friedman (1984) elaborated on its early proposal for a constant money growth rule, turning it into a plea for "freezing high-powered money."

A New Consensus?

A notable weakness of these reform plans was that they set about to cure the inflation bias of the fiat standard by suppressing the one feature that had made that standard attractive in the first place—the flexibility of response it allowed in the presence of supply and demand shocks. We have indeed seen that the degeneration of the fiat standard was not unrelated to the aim of increasing the capability of the monetary framework to cope with shocks. This aim, moreover, was not inconsistent with macroeconomic theory, which clearly indicated that a certain degree of flexibility might be desirable if the economy was exposed to exogenous uncertainty.

Not surprisingly, therefore, radical reform proposals were soon outcompeted by less ambitious ones, all hinging on the brand-new notion of credibility. Elaborating on Kydland and Prescott's seminal 1977 paper, a number of authors argued that what was really missing was an institutional mechanism for convincing private agents that the flexibility inherent in the concept of "managed money" would not be exploited either to achieve short-run, that is, transitory, welfare gains, or to pursue the private interests, such as electoral gains or seigniorage revenue, of those in charge of monetary policy. In other words, one

needed a credible framework that would make the private sector assign low probability to the event of being cheated through unexpected inflation.

In the course of the 1980s, the idea that the monetary framework that had emerged from the demise of Bretton Woods was lacking "credibility" spread so widely as to become commonplace. All standard accounts of the degeneration of the fiat standard came to rely on some form or other of Kydland and Prescott's story (see, for example, Bruno and Sachs (1985), Nordhaus (1990), and Smith (1992)). Analogously, the need to strengthen monetary institutions so as to ensure the credibility of monetary policy became a leitmotiv in central bankers' public speeches (Ciocca (1987), Volcker and Gyohten (1992)).[7]

The rise of the notion of credibility dealt a severe blow to all rule-flavored reform proposals, in that it helped to see that the announcement of rules or policy paths was in itself neither a necessary nor a sufficient condition for price stability. It was not sufficient, because announced rules were not necessarily credible. Nor was it necessary, because credibility of purpose could be achieved by directly altering the incentives faced by (or the utility function of) the policymaker. Until then, advocates of rule-based regimes had never entertained the possibility that a policy rule may be incentive incompatible, and therefore not believed by the private sector. Concern for the credibility of the restoration of the Gold Standard had been voiced in the early 1920s, but this was seen more as a contingent problem raised by the dismal state of European economies in the aftermath of the Great War than as a possible shortcoming of rule-based monetary frameworks. Be this as it may, the notion of credibility had never made its way into the theoretical literature (e.g., the notion of credibility is completely disregarded in the collection of papers on the standard edited by Yeager in the early 1960s).

While it is relatively easy to see why the notion of credibility is analytically promising, it is far less obvious how credibility can be achieved in practice. Indeed, credibility is a rather elusive notion, always in danger of turning into a truism, as has the notion of money's "acceptability." Just as one might be tempted to define a given form of money as acceptable if it is indeed ordinarily accepted as a quid pro quo, it would be equally tempting to define as credible those actions of the policymaker that are shown to have been believed by the private sector. Such an approach, however, would yield very little insight, if at all, on how to establish credibility in the first place.

---

[5]See Cooper (1982) for a review of these proposals, and Cagan (1984) for an assessment of the workings of the so-called Gold Commission.

[6]See Coats (1994) for a comprehensive survey of these schemes.

[7]The notion of credibility pertains to the *purpose* being pursued by monetary authorities, not the *outturns* of their actions. As noted by Schelling (1982), in fact, "The most a government can commit is an input, not an output—a program, not a result."

As it happens, no general theory of credibility has ever been spelled out, despite the current popularity of the term. All one can safely say, given the state of our knowledge, is that credibility can be pursued in at least three different ways (Schelling (1982)). First, a hypothetical social planner could try to devise a commitment technology, that is, a mechanism that would give those in charge of monetary policy an incentive to stick to the announced policy course. Since governments find it understandably difficult to credibly constrain themselves, this will typically take the form of a delegation of power. Second, monetary authorities could try to establish a reputation for dependability, by arranging to have their determination publicly tested at an early stage after coming into office. Finally, one could try to influence directly the private sector's expectations by increasing the visibility of the policy process, that is, by discussing, regularly and openly, the theory and the data underlying policy actions.

Clearly, these "three paths to credibility" are not mutually exclusive. For instance, even if the commitment technology were temptation proof, authorities would benefit from the private sector sharing the same theory of how the economy works, since, as noted by Schelling (1982), "translating even a confidently shared expectation of government action into a share expectation of results requires that a decisive subset of economic agents confidently shared a theory . . . relating program inputs to inflationary outputs." Conversely, even if a large section of the population shared with the authorities a given theory, there would be no guarantee that the correct actions be taken if the authorities were not working under the appropriate incentives. Elster (1989) provides further insights on credibility buildings.

In spite of its theoretical indeterminacy, the notion of credibility lies at the heart of all the reform schemes implemented in the last decade or so. Indeed, as we shall see in Section III, one can trace behind all of them the attempt to achieve credibility of purpose through delegation, reputation building, increased transparency, or a blend of these mechanisms.

III The Post–Bretton Woods Era

Against the background of the preceding discussion, we now move to reviewing the actual evolution of monetary frameworks during 1970–94.

Country Sample

Information was gathered on the evolution of monetary frameworks in 100 countries (or country unions). This country group includes almost all independent nations in existence for the 25 years covered in this paper, with the exception of countries whose monetary system was seriously disrupted by external or internal wars and countries under central planning for most of the observed period.[8] Thus, our country group does not include any of the so-called transition economies, a painful exclusion as those economies have recently become the locus of several monetary experiments (Begg (1996)). However, this drawback is offset by the advantage of working for the entire sample period with a panel of relatively homogeneous countries. Needless to say, it would be dangerous to carry over to countries introducing new currencies (as many transition economies) the experience of other countries (Selgin (1994) discusses the problems involved in introducing new fiat money).

This country group includes 22 industrial and 78 developing countries or country unions (currency unions).[9] A currency union is here considered as an individual entity distinct from its members: the monetary framework of the latter is implicit in the choice of joining a currency union, while the monetary framework of the union itself depends on the rules regulating the actions of the union's central bank. The three existing currency unions (West African Monetary Union, Central African Monetary Union, and Eastern Caribbean Currency Area) are thus included as separate entities. The countries belonging to the first two unions are also included individually. The members of the East Caribbean Currency Area were not included, as they became formally independent only after 1970.

Taxonomy of Monetary Frameworks

Monetary frameworks can, in principle, be differentiated according to three aspects: (1) whether there exist announced rules or formal institutions affecting the behavior of the monetary authorities; (2) the costs associated with repudiating announced rules; and (3) the costs of monitoring the possible deviation of the monetary authorities from announced rules. The latter are relevant because high monitoring costs favor noncompliance with the announced rules even in the absence of formal repudiation.

Our classification of monetary frameworks focuses primarily on the first aspect. In principle, this choice may bias some of the conclusions reached in this study regarding the relation among discretion, credibility and monetary frameworks, as the factors mentioned under (2) and (3) do affect the credibility of (and the degree of discretion implicit in) a certain monetary framework (Flood and Isard (1989), Lohmann (1992)). However, focusing on the first aspect has three practical advantages. First, it allows us to avoid highly subjective decisions on repudiation and monitoring costs. For example, multilateral pegs are often regarded as more costly to repudiate than unilateral pegs, as parity revisions require consensus among all countries participating in the peg (Persson and Tabellini (1994)). But Cukierman, Rodriguez, and Webb (1995) find that, in practice, unilateral pegs may have imposed equally binding constraints on monetary policies than multilateral constraints.

Second, it reduced significantly the number of potential frameworks (some of which would have included only one or two countries), thus simplifying the analysis of the main trends. For example, incorporating the difference between multilateral and unilateral pegs would have required adding three additional frameworks (corresponding to frameworks 4, 5, and 6 of Table 1).

---

[8]However, the sample includes Lebanon, as monetary policy in this country remained—only to some extent—relatively shielded from the civil war that shattered the country.

[9]The breakdown between industrial and developing countries follows the standard classification used in the IMF's *International Financial Statistics*. See Appendix for further details on the selected countries, as well as for relevant sources of information.

Table 1. A Taxonomy of Monetary Frameworks

| | Can the Monetary Authorities | | | |
| | Set short-term interest rates independently from monetary conditions abroad? | Adjust their inflation target in response to country specific shocks? | Set short-term interest rates independently from monetary conditions abroad? | Adjust their inflation target in response to country specific shocks? |
Monetary Framework	(In the short run)		(In the long run)	
Foreign currency	N	N	N	N
Currency union	N	N	N	N
Currency board	N	N	N	N
Exchange rate peg without capital controls	N	N	N	N
Exchange rate peg with capital controls and a short-term intermediate target	Y	N	N	N
Exchange rate peg with capital controls	Y	Y	N	N
Inflation targeting	Y	Y	N	N
Short-term intermediate target	Y	N	Y	Y
Discretion	Y	Y	Y	Y

Source: Appendix: Country Data.

Third, focusing also on aspects (2) and (3) would not have significantly altered the conclusions on the main trends in the evolution of monetary frameworks highlighted in the following sections. This is because there have been limited shifts of countries between frameworks differing for how easily announcements can be repudiated. In this respect, the most relevant change was the shift from Bretton Woods multilateral pegs toward bilateral pegs. But, assuming that multilateral pegs can be regarded as more costly to repudiate, this shift, if anything, strengthened the trends toward more discretionary frameworks highlighted in the following sections. As to monitoring costs, exchange rate-based frameworks are usually considered easier to monitor than monetary rules. But, as we will see, in our classification, exchange rate frameworks (with the exception of crawling pegs) are, albeit for reasons unrelated to monitoring costs, attributed a lower weight in terms of discretion than frameworks based on monetary targeting.

Thus, based on announced policy rules, nine basic monetary frameworks can be identified, which are listed in Table 1 by increasing degree of discretion. In assessing the degree of discretion, two aspects are here considered, namely whether the monetary authority (that is, the agency—the government or the central bank—in charge of monetary policy) has the possibility of (1) setting short-term interest rates independently from monetary conditions abroad and (2) surprising the private sector through unanticipated inflation without repudiating the announcements. These two aspects are considered both in the short run and in the long

run, and the table reports whether there is (Y) or there is not (N) scope for discretion under each reported framework. The relative degree of discretion of the frameworks has been assessed based on the number of yeses in the tables, and on the principle that long-term discretion is to be weighted more heavily than short-term discretion.

The first four frameworks (use of foreign currency as the only legal tender, membership in a currency union, replacement of a central bank with a currency board, and pegging the exchange rate in the absence of capital controls) leave no room for an independent monetary policy, either in the short run or in the long run, as domestic interest rates are continuously pegged, through arbitrage operations, to foreign interest rates.[10] In defining currency boards, some ambiguity is unavoidable. In principle, a currency board is characterized by the fact that 100 percent of base money creation must be matched by the acquisition of foreign exchange reserves by the central bank at a preannounced exchange rate. But, in practice, the percentage is al-

---

[10]In classifying countries as characterized by presence or absence of capital controls, we focused on whether the controls were imposed vis-à-vis the peg currency: in the absence of controls, monetary policy is dictated by that of the peg currency, even if the country maintains capital controls vis-à-vis the rest of the world. Apart from this aspect, the nature of the information on capital controls is the same as the one used in Alesina, Grilli, and Milesi-Ferretti (1993): in a given year each country was classified as having or not having capital controls based on the summary tables of the IMF's *Annual Report on Exchange Arrangements and Exchange Restrictions.*

most never 100 percent, as some limited flexibility is always admitted, at least in the very short term. This survey considers as currency boards those arrangements in which at least 90 percent of base money must be covered by foreign exchange.

The fifth framework (pegged exchange rate with capital controls and a short term intermediate monetary target) allows the monetary authority to set the stance of monetary policy in the short run independently from abroad. However, after the intermediate target is announced, monetary policy is in principle geared to the attainment of the intermediate target and cannot respond to shocks affecting the economy. Moreover, through the price-specie flow mechanism, in the long run, domestic inflation must be brought in line with foreign inflation, thus constraining the discretion of monetary policy.

The sixth framework differs from the fifth in the absence of a domestic short-term target, which increases short-run discretion.

The seventh framework (inflation targeting) has attracted much attention in recent years, particularly in industrial countries. "Inflation targeting" is not purely the announcement of some short-run inflation target by the government—something that to a different degree occurs in most countries—but the announcement of a targeted inflation path extending to a few years ahead, coupled with the setting up of procedures for public monitoring of how the monetary authorities pursue their objective.[11] Owing to medium- to long-term announced inflation targets, monetary policy has no medium- to long-term discretion. However, in the presence of flexible exchange rates to which inflation targeting is typically associated, there is room for keeping domestic monetary conditions independent from foreign monetary conditions.

The eighth framework is characterized by the announcement of a short-term intermediate target, either in the form of a monetary aggregate or of a (typically crawling) peg. This framework constrains the monetary authorities in the short run, but not in the long run, as the targets are revised periodically (at least annually).

Finally, the last framework is characterized by the lack of any announcement binding the monetary authorities (full discretion).

Before proceeding, two caveats are in order. First, the above nine frameworks do not include all monetary frameworks suggested by the economic literature. There are two remarkable omissions: the announcement of medium- to long-term intermediate

monetary targets (or of a money growth rule à la Friedman); and the announcement of nominal income targets. The reason for these omissions is the absence of practical examples of these frameworks in our country group. As discussed in Section V, monetary targeting has (almost) always been characterized by short-term announcements, rather than by the announcement of money rules. Nominal income targeting is also not a common practice, although in some cases, short-term monetary targets are explicitly derived from consistent nominal income targets. For example, it has been argued that the Bundesbank follows an income targeting procedure (Fischer (1987)). However, while in Germany monetary and income targets are defined consistently at the beginning of the planning period, during the period German monetary policy is supposed to be geared to the attainment of the monetary objective. One likely reason why nominal income targeting is not a common practice, despite its theoretical appeal (see, for example, Hall (1983), Taylor (1985), and Frankel and Chinn (1995)) is the lag with which reliable nominal income data become available even in industrial countries (Fischer (1995b)).

Second, the above classification is centered on *announced* targets or rules affecting monetary policy. The definition of *unannounced* targets—a practice followed by many central banks with respect to either exchange rates or monetary aggregates—was not considered to be relevant in this context for two reasons. First, unannounced targets cannot be monitored by the public and therefore are less binding. Second, there are theoretical reasons to believe that unannounced targets are less binding. Indeed, monetary theory has focused on the expectational effect of announcements: "tying one's hands" without announcing it is not an appropriate policy as it forgoes the advantages of flexible response to shocks, without acquiring the advantages related to the possibility of affecting expectations (see, for example, Griffiths and Wood (1981b)).[12] Thus, unannounced targets are unlikely to be as binding as announced targets. Of course, the practice of defining unpub-

---

[11]According to this definition, Israel—where the monetary authorities announce annual inflation objectives—is not included in the list of countries following an inflation targeting framework. Bufman, Leiderman, and Sokoler (1994) offer a different view.

[12]The shortcomings of not announcing binding constraints is well exemplified by the so-called Dr. Strangelove syndrome. The 1964 Stanley Kubrick movie *Dr. Strangelove, or How I Learned to Stop Worrying and Love the Bomb* focuses on the unfortunate consequences of building a device (the Doomsday machine capable of destroying "all human and animal life for one hundred years") that would be automatically set off in case of nuclear attack on the Soviet Union. The enormous deterrence of such a device arises precisely from its automatic working, which solves the time-inconsistency problem arising from the discretionary decision to counter a nuclear attack. Unfortunately, in the movie, the Soviet government delayed the announcement that the device was in operation, with catastrophic consequences.

lished monetary projections is far from useless. Many central banks use those projections to assess possible deviations of economic developments (including nonmonetary variables) from initially expected outcomes, thus deriving indications to be used to revise the setting of monetary instruments. This practice, however, corresponds to using monetary aggregates as *information variables* (in the sense defined by B. Friedman (1975) and (1990)), rather than as policy targets.

Evolution of Monetary Frameworks

Based on the detailed information reported in the Appendix, countries were classified by monetary framework for each year between 1970 and 1994. The framework assigned to each country in each year is the one prevailing for most of the year. The monetary frameworks listed in Table 1 are, in principle, mutually exclusive. In practice, however, there were a few cases of "mixed" frameworks, such as France during 1993, and the United Kingdom during 1991–92. In both cases, a (quasi) fixed exchange rate in the absence of capital controls was coupled with the announcements of money targets. In the presence of such inconsistent announcements (which in the case of France have been frequently discussed; see Icard (1994), Bryant (1994)), it has been assumed that the external target was the overriding one (de Larosière (1994)).

Table 2 summarizes the distribution of countries by monetary framework during that period. As the total sample includes 100 countries, the number of countries reported in each year/framework pair provides also the percentage of countries for the corresponding pair. In the tables referring separately to industrial and developing countries, percentages, rounded to unity, are reported in parentheses.

The following features stand out. At the beginning of the period, the "Bretton Woods order" is reflected in the overwhelming share of the fixed-exchange rate cum capital controls framework (framework 6) covering over one-half of the countries considered. Most other countries applied more binding frameworks, either by forsaking central bank activity altogether (regime 1–3) or by coupling the exchange rate con-

Table 2. Industrial and Developing Countries: Distribution by Monetary Framework

| Year | Monetary Framework | | | | | | | | |
	1	2	3	4	5	6	7	8	9
1970	6	13	2	11	2	56	0	0	10
1971	6	13	1	12	2	56	0	0	10
1972	6	13	1	13	1	54	0	1	11
1973	6	13	1	12	1	45	0	1	21
1974	4	12	1	12	1	45	0	1	24
1975	4	12	1	12	0	46	0	5	20
1976	4	12	1	12	1	42	0	6	22
1977	3	12	1	12	1	41	0	9	21
1978	3	12	1	12	1	40	0	13	18
1979	3	12	1	13	5	37	0	10	19
1980	2	12	2	10	3	38	0	13	20
1981	2	12	2	10	3	37	0	12	22
1982	2	12	2	10	3	36	0	11	24
1983	2	12	2	8	2	32	0	9	32
1984	2	13	2	8	2	30	0	10	33
1985	2	13	2	7	2	31	0	9	34
1986	2	13	2	7	2	28	0	12	34
1987	2	13	2	7	2	27	0	12	35
1988	2	13	2	7	2	27	0	14	33
1989	2	13	2	8	3	24	0	13	35
1990	2	13	2	8	4	21	1	12	37
1991	2	13	3	11	4	20	2	9	36
1992	2	13	3	12	3	19	2	12	34
1993	2	13	3	11	0	17	5	14	35
1994	2	13	3	8	1	18	5	14	36

Source: Appendix: Country Data.

straint with the absence of capital controls. Only 10 countries followed a purely discretionary approach to monetary policy. It is noticeable that currency boards—a monetary framework that has attracted much attention in recent years (Liviatan (1993))—have been used in the last 25 years very rarely, although they were more common in the 1950s and 1960s, at the time when many colonies turned into independent states. The drop from 6 to 2 in the number of countries using foreign currency (first column of Table 2) also reflects the gradual introduction of own currencies by newly independent countries.

The breakdown of the Bretton Woods regime is mirrored by the decline of countries in framework 6. However, the shift, after a sharp drop of "peggers" between 1972 and 1973, is quite gradual and continues throughout the period: initially many countries replaced the Bretton Woods multilateral peg system with bilateral pegging, or, within Europe, by alternative multilateral arrangements (first the monetary "snake," then the ERM).

The migration away from framework 6 is matched by an increase in the percentage of countries following more discretionary policies. The migration, however, follows three different phases. During the 1970s, the migration is toward both framework 8 (short-run intermediate target) and framework 9 (full discretion). Within framework 8, the announcement of monetary targets is overwhelming. Short-run exchange rate targets, in the form of an announced depreciation (or crawling peg) rate over the coming quarters, have been used in Argentina (1979–80), Brazil (1980), Chile (1978), Jamaica (1978), Portugal (1978–90), Uruguay (1979–82) and (1992–94), Mexico (1988–90), Israel (1992–94), and Colombia (1994). Unannounced crawling pegs were more common (see, for example, Williamson (1981)). During the 1980s, the number of countries using short-run intermediate targets stops increasing, while the number of countries following full discretion keeps increasing. Finally, in the 1990s, inflation targeting is virtually the only framework on the rise.

Important differences in the above trends exist between industrial and developing countries (Tables 3 and 4).[13] At the beginning of the 1970s, framework 6 was the most common one for both industrial and developing countries. However, full discretion was relatively common for industrial countries even in the early 1970s (Table 3). With the breakdown of the Bretton Woods regime, industrial countries experienced a sharp but short-lived shift toward full discretion, which was, however, rapidly replaced by ex-

change rate targets (primarily in Europe) and by short-term monetary targets. With the beginning of the 1980s, short-term monetary targets (framework 8, whose diffusion had reached 41 percent of the sample in 1980–82) became less and less popular, with their relative share dropping to 23 percent by the early 1990s. At the same time, exchange rate targets (this time coupled with free capital mobility) peaked. Their drop in 1993–94 is related to the crisis of the ERM.[14]

Developments are somewhat different for developing countries (Table 4). In the early 1970s, only a handful of developing countries (Argentina, Brazil, Korea, Lebanon, Maldives, and the Philippines, representing less than 10 percent of the total) followed a discretionary approach to monetary policy. Moreover, the shift away from framework 6 (and, more generally, from fixed exchange rate frameworks) was much more gradual than for industrial countries, as it continued at an approximately steady pace throughout the 1970s and 1980s. The announcement of short-run intermediate targets is a relatively uncommon and, if anything, new phenomenon. Inflation targeting is unknown.

Summary Indicator of the Degree of Discretion

A summary indicator of the above trends can be built by assigning to each of the nine frameworks a "weight" reflecting its degree of discretion, and by building weighted-average indexes of discretion for different country groups.

The discretion indexes in Figure 1 are built after assigning to each framework one point for each "Yes" reported in the first two columns of Table 1 and one and a half points for each "Yes" reported in the last two columns of the same table. The choice of the weight is, admittedly, largely arbitrary. However, it reflects two considerations. First, that long-term discretion involves more uncertainty on price developments than short-term discretion. Second, that the difference cannot be too large as, in many cases, the announcement of short-term targets is accompanied by an implicit commitment to monetary moderation also in the long run. In this way, long-term discretion received a higher weight than short-term discretion.

---

[13]The tables report data only for 1970, 1975, 1980, and 1985–94. Complete tables reporting all information for the period 1970–94 are available upon request from the authors.

[14]In our classification, we continued to regard as exchange rate peggers those ERM countries that, despite the widening of the ERM band to 15 percent on both sides, continued de facto to maintain the exchange rate within the old 2.25 percent band for most of 1994.

Table 3. Industrial Countries: Distribution by Monetary Framework
(Number of countries and percentage composition)

Framework	1970	1975	1980	1985	1986	1987	1988	1989	1990	1991	1992	1993	1994
1	0	0	0	0	0	0	0	0	0	0	0	0	0
	(0)	(0)	(0)	(0)	(0)	(0)	(0)	(0)	(0)	(0)	(0)	(0)	(0)
2	0	0	0	0	0	0	0	0	0	0	0	0	0
	(0)	(0)	(0)	(0)	(0)	(0)	(0)	(0)	(0)	(0)	(0)	(0)	(0)
3	0	0	0	0	0	0	0	0	0	0	0	0	0
	(0)	(0)	(0)	(0)	(0)	(0)	(0)	(0)	(0)	(0)	(0)	(0)	(0)
4	3	2	3	3	3	4	4	4	5	8	9	8	5
	(14)	(9)	(14)	(14)	(14)	(18)	(18)	(18)	(23)	(36)	(41)	(36)	(23)
5	1	0	3	2	2	2	2	3	3	3	3	0	0
	(5)	(0)	(14)	(9)	(9)	(9)	(9)	(14)	(14)	(14)	(14)	(0)	(0)
6	14	9	5	5	5	5	4	4	3	1	2	1	1
	(64)	(41)	(23)	(23)	(23)	(23)	(18)	(18)	(14)	(5)	(9)	(5)	(5)
7	0	0	0	0	0	0	0	0	1	2	2	5	5
	(0)	(0)	(0)	(0)	(0)	(0)	(0)	(0)	(5)	(9)	(9)	(23)	(23)
8	0	5	8	7	7	6	7	6	6	4	4	4	5
	(0)	(23)	(36)	(32)	(32)	(27)	(32)	(27)	(27)	(18)	(18)	(18)	(23)
9	4	6	3	5	5	5	5	5	4	4	2	4	6
	(18)	(27)	(14)	(23)	(23)	(23)	(23)	(23)	(18)	(18)	(9)	(18)	(27)

Source: Appendix: Country Data.

Table 4. Developing Countries: Distribution by Monetary Framework
(Number of countries and percentage composition)

Framework	1970	1975	1980	1985	1986	1987	1988	1989	1990	1991	1992	1993	1994
1	6	4	2	2	2	2	2	2	2	2	2	2	2
	(8)	(5)	(3)	(3)	(3)	(3)	(3)	(3)	(3)	(3)	(3)	(3)	(3)
2	13	12	12	13	13	13	13	13	13	13	13	13	13
	(17)	(15)	(15)	(17)	(17)	(17)	(17)	(17)	(17)	(17)	(17)	(17)	(17)
3	2	1	2	2	2	2	2	2	2	3	3	3	3
	(3)	(1)	(3)	(3)	(3)	(3)	(3)	(3)	(3)	(4)	(4)	(4)	(4)
4	8	10	7	4	4	3	3	4	3	3	3	3	3
	(10)	(13)	(9)	(5)	(5)	(4)	(4)	(5)	(4)	(4)	(4)	(4)	(4)
5	1	0	0	0	0	0	0	0	1	1	0	0	1
	(1)	(0)	(0)	(0)	(0)	(0)	(0)	(0)	(1)	(1)	(0)	(0)	(1)
6	42	37	33	26	23	22	23	20	18	19	17	16	17
	(54)	(47)	(42)	(33)	(29)	(28)	(29)	(26)	(23)	(24)	(22)	(21)	(22)
7	0	0	0	0	0	0	0	0	0	0	0	0	0
	(0)	(0)	(0)	(0)	(0)	(0)	(0)	(0)	(0)	(0)	(0)	(0)	(0)
8	0	0	5	2	5	6	7	7	6	5	8	10	9
	(0)	(0)	(6)	(3)	(6)	(8)	(9)	(9)	(8)	(6)	(10)	(13)	(12)
9	6	14	17	29	29	30	28	30	33	32	32	31	30
	(8)	(18)	(22)	(37)	(37)	(38)	(36)	(38)	(42)	(41)	(41)	(40)	(38)

Source: Appendix: Country Data.

The figure reports the weighted average degree of discretion by country groups using as weights the number of countries adopting each framework. In doing so, each country is treated as equally important, regardless of its population or income size. This approach was followed because we are mainly interested in studying trends in the behavior of policy authorities, rather than in deriving a "world index of monetary discretion." However, the indexes in this figure were also recomputed by weighing each country based on relative GDP (at PPP in 1989). The income-weighted indexes move in line with those of the figure for both industrial and developing countries. Quite obviously, the income-weighted index for the whole sample follows closely the movement of the index for industrial countries (the correlation coefficient is 0.86), albeit at a higher level of discretion, reflecting the relatively higher level of discretion of the three major economies.

The figure suggests that, primarily as a consequence of the shift away from exchange rate anchors, monetary discretion has, on the average of all countries, increased in the last 25 years. The trend is, however, particularly strong in the first 17 years, while in the last period, the index seems to have stabilized. The figure also shows that, owing to the composition of the sample, the total average follows very much the movements of the developing countries' index. The discretion index for industrial countries jumps in 1973–74, but then declines slightly through the end of the 1980s. After dropping dramatically in 1991–92 (reflecting the capital movement liberalization in European countries in the context of pegged exchange rates), it increases again in 1993–94 (ERM crisis).

Another feature highlighted by Figure 1 is that, with the exception of 1991–92, the average degree of discretion is higher in industrial than in develop-

Figure 1. Monetary Discretion Index

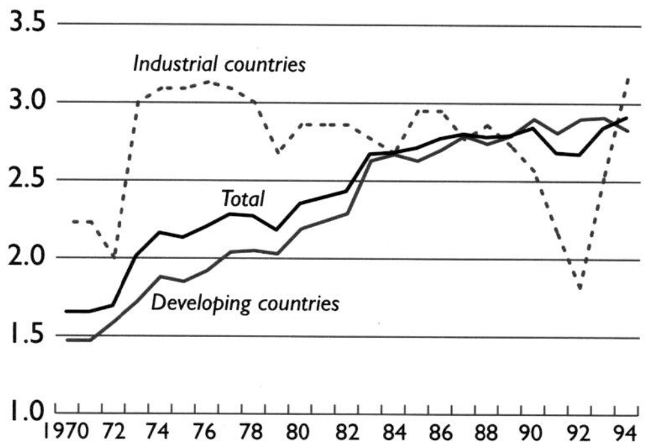

Source: Appendix: Country Data.

ing countries. However, the difference seems to have narrowed significantly during the 1970s and early 1980s.

Frameworks During Disinflations

It has been argued that the choice of monetary framework is influenced by inflationary conditions. For example, Bernanke and Mishkin (1992) argue that "central bankers are more likely to adopt targets for monetary growth, or to increase their emphasis on meeting existing targets, when inflation is perceived as the number one problem." If this were the case, it could be argued that the trend toward greater discretion may be related to the decline of inflation observed since the early 1980s, at least in the indus-

Table 5. Breaking the Inflation Momentum
(High level and hyperinflations)

Country	Stabilization Period	Initial Inflation	Final Inflation	Framework
Ghana	1983–85	122.6	10.3	9
Bolivia	1985–89	11,749.6	15.2	9
Israel	1985–88	304.6	16.3	6
Mexico	1988–92	114.2	15.5	8[1]
Uganda	1988–93	196.1	6.1	9
Argentina	1990–94	2,314.0	4.2	3
Peru	1990–94	7,481.8	23.7	9

Source: Appendix: Country Data.
[1]Framework 6 in 1992.

Table 6. Breaking the Inflation Momentum
(Moderate inflation)

Country	Stabilization Period	Initial Inflation	Final Inflation	Framework
India	1974–78	28.6	2.5	6
Japan	1974–78	23.1	4.1	9
Malaysia	1974–75	17.3	4.5	9
Singapore	1974–75	22.4	2.6	9
Thailand	1974–76	24.3	4.1	6
Saudi Arabia	1975–78	23.6	−1.6	4
Côte d'Ivoire[1]	1979–83	16.3	5.9	2
Dominican Republic	1980–83	16.8	4.8	6
Honduras	1980–84	18.1	4.7	6
Malta	1980–83	15.7	−0.9	6
Mauritius[1]	1980–83	42.0	5.6	6[2]
Thailand	1980–83	19.7	3.7	6
United Kingdom	1980–83	18.0	4.6	8
United States	1980–83	13.5	3.1	8
Venezuela	1980–83	21.5	6.3	2[3]
Korea	1980–83	28.7	3.4	8
Togo	1981–84	19.7	−3.5	2
Ireland	1982–86	17.1	3.8	6
Italy	1982–86	16.5	5.8	5
Kenya	1982–86	20.7	4.8	9
Philippines	1984–86	50.3	0.8	9
New Zealand	1987–91	15.7	2.6	9
Jordan	1989–92	26.7	4.0	6
Dominican Republic	1990–92	59.4	4.0	9
Iceland	1990–92	15.5	4.0	9[4]

Source: Appendix: Country Data.

[1]"Borderline case" for which the definition of "successful disinflation" repeated in the text does not strictly apply because inflation did not fall below 5 percent.

[2]Framework 9 in 1993.

[3]Framework 9 in 1983.

[4]Framework 7 in 1990.

discretion may be related to the decline of inflation observed since the early 1980s, at least in the industrial world.[15] To explore this possibility, we have focused on the monetary framework of countries that undertook successful stabilizations. There is a second reason to focus on these countries, namely that in these countries the formal monetary framework is likely to be taken more seriously than in countries with high inflation. For example, in countries with high inflation, the constraint imposed by exchange rate pegs may be watered down by frequent parity revisions or by increasingly tight exchange rate controls.[16]

In defining stabilizations, we distinguish between high inflations (hyperinflations) and moderate inflations. Successful stabilizations are respectively defined as achieving a reduction of the CPI inflation rate from above 100 percent to below 20 percent in 4 years and from above 15 percent to below 5 percent in 4 years.[17]

There are only a few cases of stabilizations from inflation levels over 100 percent (Table 5, on previous page), and they all concentrate in a relatively short time span, which prevents any analysis of the evolution of monetary frameworks. In four of the seven cases considered here, a discretionary frame-

---

[15]The evidence on inflation performance in developing countries is more mixed (see Baliño and Cottarelli (1994)).

[16]Note that we are *not* addressing the issue of which framework is more appropriate to disinflate the economy, an issue that would require comparing the cost of disinflation under different frameworks (see, among others, De Grauwe (1989) and Chadha, Masson, and Meredith (1992)).

[17]All definitions of "successful disinflations" are somewhat arbitrary (see Bruno (1991) for an alternative definition). To alleviate this problem, we have included in our sample some borderline cases (see Tables 5 and 6).

[18]Admittedly, the sample considered in Table 5 is quite limited. Végh (1992), looking at a broader spectrum of cases covering the last 70 years, concludes that an exchange rate peg is crucial in stopping hyperinflations. Nevertheless, reference to episodes too far back in time may not be entirely relevant, owing to changes in

The number of stabilizations from moderate inflation is higher (Table 6) and allows the computation of a discretion index based on the same methodology followed above (Figure 2). The index is based on all-year framework pairs reported in Table 6. Each country was included in the computation only during the disinflation years. As this index is computed on a more limited sample, it has a strong erratic component (and was not computable for some periods). Nevertheless, there seems to be a clear trend toward discretion, if anything more pronounced than the one observed for the total country sample.

---

the institutional environment. In this respect, it could be noted that in all of the above cases in which a discretionary framework was adopted, the credibility of disinflation was buttressed by IMF-support to the stabilization program (see Section IV).

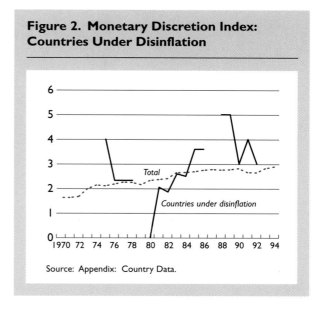

Figure 2. Monetary Discretion Index: Countries Under Disinflation

Source: Appendix: Country Data.

IV Credibility Cum Discretion

The shift toward greater discretion observed over the last 25 years may appear (at first view) somewhat disturbing, given the increased recognition in the economic literature that credibility is an important component of a low inflation environment. But, as stressed in Section II, credible frameworks and rule-based frameworks are quite different things. The key to success is to set in place arrangements so that the private sector will believe that the margins of instrument flexibility left to the monetary authorities by relatively relaxed monetary frameworks will not be used to exploit the short-run trade-off between inflation and output, or to raise seigniorage revenues. Here are discussed four strategies to attain credibility at the cost of no or limited loss of flexibility, which have become increasingly common in the last 25 years. Two of these strategies—granting instrument independence to the central bank and relying on IMF-supported programs amount respectively to modifying incentives or preferences through institutional action and to submitting key economic policy decisions to the scrutiny of an external agency with a well-established distaste for inflation. As Briault, Haldane, and King (1996) remark, the third strategy—inflation targeting—with its emphasis on accountability and transparency, aims at achieving credibility by words, while the fourth strategy—building an anti-inflationary reputation—amounts to revealing information about the authorities' preferences by deeds.

The discussion will also highlight that differences in the economic and institutional environment, by shaping the feasibility set for monetary reform, go a long way toward explaining why credibility of purpose has been pursued in certain ways. The reason is that in a fiat standard, announcements about monetary policy run into a serious problem of enforcement—the main potential villain being also the ultimate enforcer. In these circumstances, as Elster (1995) aptly remarks, in order to attain credibility, the precommitting agency must of necessity act through the external environment. A resolute inner stance or a mere announcement will simply not do. We disagree, however, with McCallum's (1996) remark to the effect that "if a precommitment technol-ogy does not exist, then it does not exist and no arrangement can entirely escape that fact." Indeed, monetary history is replete with examples of institutional adaptation designed to constrain the monetary powers of the sovereign under changing circumstances. The experience of the last 25 years is no exception in that respect.

However, the external environment may vary markedly across countries. Thus, certain institutions, such as a truly independent central bank, are feasible only at specific levels of economic and institutional development. As Fischer (1995a) suggests, it makes little sense to provide for the legal independence of the central bank in countries where the law is flouted and where financial markets are undeveloped, if not altogether missing. Moreover, policymakers operating under a regime of political dictatorship or lacking an efficient financial sector that would rapidly sanction financial profligacy might find it insurmountably hard to precommit themselves even if they wanted to (Elster (1995)).[19] Thus, in countries where "domestic delegation" is not feasible, it may be inevitable to search for an external source of credibility. Indeed, our data show that many developing and, in some cases, nondemocratic countries have been able to precommit themselves by submitting their economic policies to the conditionality implicit in IMF-supported programs.

Central Bank Independence

Probably the most visible institutional development associated with the current wave of monetary reform has been the revision of the role and status of the central bank. In the space of seven years, from 1989 to 1995, seven countries in the industrial group and ten in the developing group have significantly altered the legal framework within which the

---

[19]Elster quotes China in the 1980s as a case in point, arguing that, while Chinese leaders may well have wanted to precommit themselves to a hands-off policy, "there was no way to do so credibly, because as they had all the power, they were unable to make themselves *unable* to interfere" (Elster (1995), p. 215).

central bank operates (Table 7). At the time of writing, a number of other countries are in the process of doing the same. The revision has hinged on three pillars. The first has been a more precise definition of the central bank's mission, with greater emphasis on the objective of price stability, in many cases indicated as the overriding objective of the central bank's actions. The second has been a considerable widening of the degree of independence of the central bank from political pressure. In particular, the central banks whose status has been modified have generally been freed from any obligation to finance either the government or government-controlled bodies and have been given sole responsibility for setting policy instruments.[20] Finally, greater emphasis has been laid on the means and forms through which the central bank accounts for its actions ex post.

The tendency toward greater central bank independence and accountability has certainly been magnified by the Maastricht Treaty, which elevated the above principles to the rank of prerequisites for joining the European Economic and Monetary Union. However, one could argue that the current reforms of central banks would have been impressive even without the Treaty, the more so since our sample does not include Eastern European countries, where the phenomenon has reached sizable proportions as well. To find a comparable switch in the two-century long history of central banks, one must go back at least to the wave of nationalizations that marked the late 1930s and early 1940s (De Kock (1974)), if not to the mid-nineteenth century, when the model set by the British Bank Charter Act of 1844 rapidly spread throughout the Western World (Giannini (1995)).

There is a notable difference, though. In both previous instances, the aim of the reform was to reduce the degree of discretion allotted to the central bank. This was done, in the mid-nineteenth century, by setting very strict rules on the issue of banknotes, and, in the nationalization era, by subjecting the central bank management to the directives and control of political institutions. This time, instead, the reform has resulted, as stated above, in greater operational discretion of the central bank in the pursuit of its statutory goals.

Whether this kind of Copernican Revolution will last remains to be seen, of course. The strategy is clearly reminiscent of the Rogoff-Tabellini-Persson version of the delegation story, according to which a socially preferable equilibrium can be achieved by delegating authority over monetary policy to an in-

dependent central bank managed by a "conservative" central banker, that is, by someone who puts a higher weight on inflation (relative to employment) than society in its loss function.[21] More than on its theoretical plausibility, however, the case for central bank independence seems to have been predicated on two bits of evidence. The first has to do with the fact that central bank independence, while negatively related to inflation, at least in the industrial countries (Cukierman (1992)), apparently has had no cost in terms of growth, or growth variability (Alesina and Summers (1993)), thus coming to be seen as a free lunch from a macroeconomic perspective. The second has been the truly remarkable performance in recent decades of the German economy, featuring at the same time what is arguably the most independent central bank in the world and the best inflation performance and comparatively high rates of growth in the industrial world.

Inflation Targeting or Increasing Transparency

Altering the legal status of the central bank reflects the attempt to establish credibility of monetary policy by modifying by law the incentive structure, or the utility function, of the policymaker. A number of industrial countries have found this path to credibility unattractive on two counts. First, it may be politically undesirable, or simply unfeasible, to concentrate so much power in the hands of nonelected officials. Second, the inverse correlation between actual inflation and the degree of independence of the central bank may in a longer-run perspective turn out to be spurious.

Indeed, critics of the concept of central bank independence often point out that, on the one hand, a distaste for inflation has in some cases predated the enhancement of central bank independence. For instance, in New Zealand, inflation fell from 16 percent to 6 percent before any change in legislation was enacted. Analogously, in Italy, inflation fell in the course of the 1980s from above 20 percent to less than 5 percent, while the first legislated steps toward enhanced central bank independence were taken only in the early 1990s. Similar stories could be told for other countries (Pollard (1993)). On the other hand, a commitment to low inflation by an independent central banker may lack credibility if the announced policy ostensibly conflicts with other government policies.

---

[20]See Cottarelli (1993) for a discussion of the relation between central bank independence and constraints on central bank credit to the government.

[21]See Rogoff (1985a). As Persson and Tabellini (1994) remark, "conservationism" could be imposed on the central bank by legislating that the main objective of monetary policy should be that of stabilizing the price level.

Table 7. Recent Changes in Central Bank Legislation

Country	Year of Reform	Year of Previous Major Change	Main Changes Introduced
Industrial countries			
Belgium	1993	1939	The 1993 Act states that the government cannot oppose a decision taken by the central bank relating to its key tasks, i.e., the implementation of monetary and foreign exchange policy, the management of foreign reserves, and the promotion of the smooth operation of the payments system. The act also prohibits the extension of credit by the central bank to the government.
France	1993	1945	Under the 1993 Act, the central bank "shall formulate and implement monetary policy with the aim of ensuring price stability" (Art. 1). The central bank "shall neither seek nor accept instructions from the government or any person in the performance of its duties" (Art. 1). Under previous legislation, the government was responsible for formulating monetary policy, whereas the bank was only responsible for its implementation. Credit to the government is forbidden. Authority over monetary policy is now attributed to a nine-member monetary policy committee, chaired by the central bank's governor.
Greece	1992	1982	According to the 1992 Act, the central bank is prohibited, starting from January 1992, from extending credit to the government. The central bank, however, still formulates and implements monetary policy on the basis of the government administrative guidelines and macroeconomic objectives.
Italy	1992–93	1936	The 1992 Act grants the governor the power to set the official discount rate, previously set by the minister of the treasury at the proposal of the governor. The 1993 Law prohibits the extension of credit to the government by the central bank and grants the central bank the power to set banks' reserve requirements. The objective to be pursued by the central bank—in accordance with Article 47 of the Italian Constitution, but not stated in the latter's statute nor in the law—is taken to be the maintenance of monetary stability.
New Zealand	1989	1936	According to the Reserve Bank Act of 1989, "the primary function of the Bank is to formulate and implement monetary policy directed to the economic objectives of achieving and maintaining stability in the general price level." The target rate of inflation is jointly determined by the treasury and the central bank. While the bank has the sole authority to formulate and implement monetary policy, a formal "override" provision exists whereby the government may change this policy.
Portugal	1990–95	1974–75	Under the 1990 Act, central bank credit to the government was limited; the act was amended in 1993 to eliminate any form of direct credit to the government. The September 1995 amendment mandated the bank to mantain price stability as its primary objective.
Spain	1994	1938	According to the 1994 Act, the central bank "shall define and implement monetary policy with the primary objective of achieving price stability" (Art. 7). The central bank "shall pursue its activities and fulfill its objectives with the autonomy from the administration" (Art. 1), but, without prejudice to the objective of price stability, the central bank's "monetary policy shall support the general economic policy of the government" (Art. 7). Under previous legislation, the central bank was "to conduct monetary policy both domestically and externally in accordance with the general objectives set by the government." The 1994 Act also prohibits the extension of credit to the public sector by the central bank.

Developing countries[1]

Country			
Argentina	1992	1946–49	In 1992, the Central Bank Law was amended to conform with the Convertibility Law of October 1992, which committed the central bank to sell foreign currency at a fixed exchange rate and maintain at all times unrestricted international reserves in an amount not less than 100 percent of base money.
Chile	1989	1953	The Organic Law of 1993 specifies that the objectives of the central bank are "the stability of the currency system" and "the due payment of internal and foreign debts." Since 1975, the formulation of monetary and exchange rate policy is the responsibility of a five-member monetary council chaired by the central bank's president.
Colombia	1991–92	1926	The December 31, 1992 Law, based on the 1991 Constitution, mandated the central bank "to maintain the purchasing power of the currency." Moreover, it raised the legal status of the central bank to that of an independent public entity, granted full autonomy in the use of monetary instruments, and confirmed the tight ceilings on central bank credit to the government introduced by the 1991 Constitution.
Honduras	1995	...	As part of the IMF-supported adjustment program, the government is preparing draft legislation to grant higher autonomy to the central bank, and to recapitalize the central bank.
Israel	1985	1954	The 1985 amendment to the 1954 Law—known as the "prohibition of printing money law" (see Bank of Israel (1991), page 25)—introduced very tight constraints on central bank credit to the government.
Mexico	1993	1985	The Ley del Banco de México of December 23, 1993 redefines as the bank's primary objective the pursuit of the "currency's purchasing power stability" and sets as secondary objective "promoting the financial system's sound development and the proper functioning of the payment system." Moreover, the law redefines the provisions concerning central bank credit to the government, introducing more stringent procedures for their enforcement.
Pakistan	1994	1956	The 1994 amendments substantially increased the State Bank of Pakistan's autonomy by widening the powers of its board, and strengthening the position of its members. However, the government still retains primary responsibilities for the formulation of monetary policy.
Peru	1992	...	The December 30, 1992 Ley Orgánica del Banco Central de Reserva del Perú mandated the central bank to pursue monetary stability as its only objective. Moreover, it prohibited all forms of direct credit to the government and severely constrained the purchase of government securities on secondary markets.
Philippines	1993	1950	The new Central Bank Act defines as the primary objective of the central bank "to maintain price stability conducive to a balanced and sustainable growth of the economy" and, as the secondary objective, to "promote and maintain monetary stability and the convertibility of the peso"; the act also strengthens independence from the government as well as the bank's financial position.
South Africa	1989	1944	According to the 1987 revision of the central bank statutes, the primary objective of the bank is "the pursuit of monetary stability and balanced economic growth in the republic." However, there exists no formal division of monetary responsibilities between the bank and the government.
Uganda	1993	1966	The new Bank of Uganda Act mandated the Bank of Uganda to "maintain monetary stability," within a broader objective of "achieving and maintaining economic stability." The bank was given primary responsibility for formulating and implementing monetary policy (although the government also retains some responsibilities). Moreover, the act set legal ceilings on central bank credit to the government and strengthened the financial independence of the bank.
Venezuela	1992	1939	The 1992 revision of central bank legislation aimed at increasing the autonomy of the bank. It is now stated explicitly that monetary stability is one of the main objectives of the bank. To this end, the law grants extensive powers to the bank to regulate interest rates and bank reserves. The law also prohibits the bank from granting direct credits to the national government and from guaranteeing the obligations of the republic.

Sources: Eijffinger and Schaling (1993); Lindgren and Dueñas (1994); Capie, Goodhart, and Schnadt (1994); Bank of Japan (1995); and Eijffinger and van Keulen (1995).

[1]Only countries whose central bank legislation has undergone significant changes are shown in this table.

Since, as seen in Section II, one may trace the inflation bias of the fiat standard back to agents' uncertainty (or misinformation) about the true intentions of monetary authorities, greater transparency of the policymaking process has appeared an obvious alternative to altering the institutional structure. As pointed out by Briault, Haldane, and King (1996), transparency, in addition to revealing information on the authorities' inflation preferences, may also be useful in revealing the authorities' model of how the economy works, thereby leading to greater social welfare.

A concern for transparency is easily detectable in countries that have espoused inflation targeting, in rapid rise in recent years (Table 2). For example, ever since inflation targets have been adopted by the U.K. government, in 1992, the Bank of England has published a quarterly report containing a detailed record of the authorities' performance in controlling inflation. In addition, since April 1994, the minutes of the key monthly meetings between the Chancellor and the Governor of the central bank have been made available to the public (Ammer and Freeman (1995)). Similarly, in Sweden, the Riksbank publishes three times a year its inflation report (Svensson (1995)); quarterly assessments of economic developments and inflation are also published by the Bank of Finland (Åkerholm and Brunila (1995)), which has also recently started publishing its inflation forecast. In Canada, though no inflation report is published, the central bank has striven ever since the inflation targeting regime has been adopted to bolster the standing of price stability as a policy goal and the overall credibility of monetary policy through regular press releases and other publications (Ammer and Freeman (1995)).

In some of the above countries, influential proposals for reforming the legislation governing the central bank put forward by parliamentary committees have been spurned. This suggests that inflation and central bank independence should not be regarded as necessary components of one and the same strategy, as Leiderman and Svensson (1995) seem to argue. New Zealand may be counted as the one exception to this proposition, since the 1989 Reform Act at once mandated central bank independence, the adoption of inflation targeting and explicit procedures for disclosing information about the conduct of monetary policy. Even in the case of New Zealand, though, there is some debate as to whether the 1989 Act actually resulted in greater central bank independence, given that under current legislation, the government has the right to participate in the setting of the inflation target, the faculty to override the central bank, and the power to dismiss the governor if he fails to fulfill his goals.

IMF Conditionality

As noted in Section IV, empirical research has established a clear negative empirical correlation between central bank independence and inflation performance in industrial countries. However, the same relation does not seem to hold in developing countries (Cukierman (1992)). Several explanations have been suggested to account for this phenomenon. Fischer (1995b), for example, blames it on imperfect law enforcement in many developing countries and on the involvement of the central bank in the financing of government deficits, a feature common to many central banks in the developing world irrespective of their nominal independence. Mas (1995) mentions shallow financial markets as an additional factor constraining the actual room for maneuver of monetary policy in developing countries. Notably, both sets of factors would equally undermine any attempt to establish credibility by resorting to inflation targeting.

By no means, however, does all this imply that developing countries have no option other than to remain stuck in a low-credibility, high-inflation equilibrium or accept a severe limitation of instrument flexibility (as in the case of an exchange rate peg). Both theory and past experience suggest that the authorities in these countries can enhance the credibility of a disinflationary effort by "delegating" policy responsibilities to an international enforcer.[22]

In this respect, Figure 3 highlights the strong time correlation between the number of developing countries included in framework 9 (full discretion) and the number of countries with IMF-supported programs in place (the correlation index is 0.83 on levels and 0.28 on first differences). There is a clear, and even stronger, increase in the share of program countries among those involved in disinflation policies (Figure 4). Is there a relation between these trends? We believe so, because of the role that IMF programs can play as a credibility-augmenting device.

Fund programs are based on the concept of conditionality (Guitián (1979) and (1995)), a term used to indicate that loans are granted provided governments

---

[22]The term "delegation" is here used in a loose sense. As detailed below, Fund conditionality involves the agreement between the Fund and country authorities on certain policy actions and the identification of clear financial consequences if certain performance criteria are not met. A much more extensive form of delegation accompanied the loans arranged under the aegis of the League of Nations in the aftermath of World War I. At the time, the concept implied more or less explicitly a limitation of sovereignty for the countries concerned, as typically the syndicated loans arranged by the League were often predicated not only on the adoption of sound macroeconomic policies and structural reforms, but also on the appointment of League-sponsored officials (often foreign bankers) to key posts in the country's public administration.

follow certain macroeconomic policies. These policies are monitored and assessed against a set of criteria, referring to a combination of what could be considered as final policy targets (foreign exchange reserves) and intermediate targets (such as domestic credit expansion and domestic credit to the government). These targets, however, are not fully disclosed to the public. What is typically announced through press releases is that the IMF has agreed to extend credit to a country, together with some broad information on the main macroeconomic targets (GDP growth, inflation, public deficit-to-GDP ratio, and, sometimes, targeted reserve-to-import ratio). While IMF programs can be as short as one year, it is quite common that a new arrangement comes into operation when the old one expires. Moreover, multiyear programs have become increasingly common. For example, at the end of 1994, about three-fourths of the outstanding programs had a duration of over one year (and about 60 percent of at least three years).

What are the implications of such an arrangement in terms of instrument flexibility? Contrary to what is sometimes believed, IMF programs involve a fairly high degree of instrument flexibility. First, it is remarkable that the monetary discretion index of countries with IMF programs is significantly higher than the average (Figure 5). The difference is significantly lower in the most recent period but this is entirely due to the need for IMF-financing of CFA countries (which, as members of currency unions, have a fairly low level of monetary discretion). Excluding these countries, the difference remains broadly constant throughout the period. To a large extent this is because, again contrary to common wisdom, exchange rate pegs are not an integral component of IMF programs:[23] during 1970–94, exchange rate pegs were used on average in about 55 percent of IMF programs, while in the same period the relative frequency of pegs in developing countries was about 73 percent.

As to the performance criteria set by the program, Guitián (1994a) notes that:

> it is of course advisable to supplement quantified policy action with an opportunity to exercise judgement, that is, an opportunity to assess the validity of the agreed quantitative policy commitments. This supplement is always included in IMF programs in the form of so called *review clauses*. These clauses call for consultations between the member and the institution to evaluate, inter alia, the appropriate-

[23]For example, Krugman (1995) lists a pegged exchange rate as one key component of the economic policies inspired by the so-called Washington consensus, an expression coined by John Williamson to refer to the views of the Washington-based international organizations.

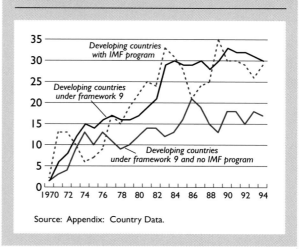

Figure 3. Number of Developing Countries with IMF-Supported Program and Under Framework 9

Source: Appendix: Country Data.

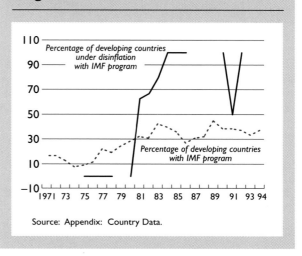

Figure 4. Percentage of Developing Countries Under Disinflation with IMF Program

Source: Appendix: Country Data.

ness of the quantified criteria and reach understandings on the circumstances under which modifications or adaptations are warranted.

Thus, IMF programs allow, in principle, the Fund and the program country to agree on changes in the program design to take into account more updated information on recent economic developments, including shifts in behavioral parameters (such as the demand for money). Program reviews tend to be quite

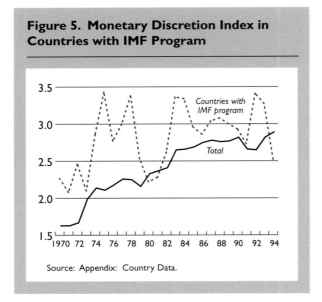

Figure 5. Monetary Discretion Index in Countries with IMF Program

Source: Appendix: Country Data.

frequent (usually quarterly or twice a year), thus allowing for a substantial amount of flexibility and discretion. Moreover, the breaching of performance criteria can be waived at the discretion of the Board of Directors. This typically occurs "in situations of small or reversible deviations" (Guitián (1995)).

More discretion, however, need not impair credibility. The reason is that the agency in charge of assessing the desirability of deviating from the initially defined targets (the International Monetary Fund) does not benefit from those deviations.[24] In other words, as in the case of Rogoff's conservative central banker, the IMF Board's utility function tends to differ from the average utility function of the country in question. Thus, for example, the (domestic and international) public knows that the Fund will not agree to accommodate a monetary expansion aimed at temporarily boosting employment, as the Fund (which is interested in recovering the resources invested in the country) will not benefit from such an expansion. In this respect, while Fund arrangements may be as short as one year, the repayment period extends to several years beyond the program period. Thus, there is a natural concern for the long-run evolution of the country.

The increased number of IMF programs is related to a number of reasons whose analysis goes beyond the scope of this paper. Nevertheless, this increase is likely to have satisfied to some extent the need for credibility that is inherent in monetary policymaking

and which in the past had been satisfied primarily by pegging the exchange rate. Indeed, Figure 3 also shows that the increase in the number of countries following a discretion-based monetary policy (framework 9) is much more contained after excluding those under an IMF program.

There is, in principle, a constraint on the role that IMF programs can play to enhance monetary credibility. A condition for an IMF program is the existence of a balance of payments need, rather than the pursuit of price stability. Thus, in principle, a country that does not have a balance of payments need cannot use Fund arrangements as a credibility-enhancing device. However, this problem is often of little practical consequence. In reality, balance of payments disequilibria and inflationary pressures tend to be combined. Moreover, empirical evidence confirms that the role of the Fund as provider of credibility, rather than as provider of balance of payments resources, has increased considerably, particularly in the last 10 years.

In this respect, Figure 6 reports the ratio between actual and potential borrowing for all Fund arrangements during 1955–95. Fund arrangements involve the opening of a line of credit from which countries can draw, with repayments starting only after the expiration of the arrangement. The figure refers to the simple average, across arrangements, of the ratio between the outstanding stock of drawings at the time when the arrangement expired and the amount of the line of credit (that is the maximum amount of drawings). The average for each year refers to the arrangements that were initiated in a certain year. This ratio, which had increased rapidly in the early 1980s as a result of the debt crisis, dropped dramatically in the second half of the 1980s, while at the same time the number of arrangements remained high or even increased (Figure 3). This is an indication that countries turned increasingly to the Fund to enhance the credibility of their policies, rather than for borrowing.

Investing in Reputation

As emphasized by McCallum (1995), a discretion-based approach does not necessarily lead to a higher inflation equilibrium if the monetary authority recognizes the futility of trying to fool systematically the private sector, and as a consequence the benefits that can be drawn from an anti-inflationary reputation. Most theoretical treatments of the subject, however, conclude that reputational equilibria may prove hard to establish and even harder to maintain. As it turns out, the required initial investment in reputation may be quite demanding in terms of forgone output; even if the authorities were willing and able to make it, the strategy would be workable only if

---

[24]The credibility effect related to IMF monitoring of domestic economic policies is formally analyzed in Dominguez (1993). See also Anayiotos (1994).

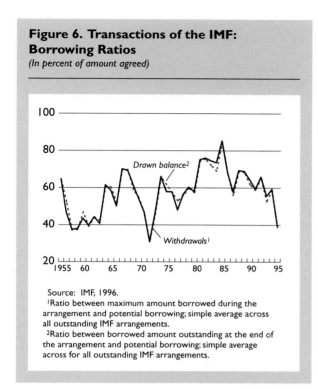

Figure 6. Transactions of the IMF: Borrowing Ratios
(In percent of amount agreed)

Source: IMF, 1996.
[1]Ratio between maximum amount borrowed during the arrangement and potential borrowing; simple average across all outstanding IMF arrangements.
[2]Ratio between borrowed amount outstanding at the end of the arrangement and potential borrowing; simple average across for all outstanding IMF arrangements.

they heavily discounted the future and if the reversion to high inflationary expectations in case of even a single instance of "cheating" could be expected to last long enough (Persson and Tabellini (1994)).

Thus, in point of theory, one should expect reputational equilibria to be attractive only in a small set of countries, namely those (1) whose economy is robust enough to be able to absorb any short-run loss of output resulting from the frontloaded investment in anti-inflationary reputation; (2) that have already delegated to a large extent monetary powers to a central bank whose planning horizon can be expected to be longer than that of elected governments; and (3) where a well-developed and reactive financial sector is capable of punishing the authorities for cheating.

Our data set seems broadly to confirm this prediction. In 1994, there were 22 countries characterized by full discretion (framework 9) and absence of Fund programs. However, many of these countries entered this group only recently. The group includes, for example, Costa Rica, Tunisia, and the Dominican Republic (which recently ended an IMF-supported program), Trinidad and Tobago (which shifted to a flexible exchange rate only recently), Turkey (which had an IMF program in place starting in July 1994), Brazil (which in the second half of 1994 introduced an exchange rate based stabilization program), Denmark and Portu-

gal (orphans of the exchange rate mechanism), and Zaïre[25] (where the shift to discretion was accompanied by hyperinflation). In Portugal and Denmark, the exchange rate constraint is still regarded as the main policy objective, even if in reality the fluctuations around the parity remained relatively large in 1993–94. The hard core group of countries that has practiced full discretion for a number of years includes only 12 countries: Australia, Indonesia, Japan,[26] Lebanon,[27] Malaysia, Mauritius, the Maldives, Paraguay, Singapore, Taiwan, Western Samoa, and the United States. In addition, quite a few of these countries seem to have joined the group more as a result of institutional inertia than out of reputational considerations. For example, some of its members (Paraguay and Western Samoa) did experience relatively high (and variable) inflation rates. Others, like the Maldives, experienced at some stage a sharp deterioration in overall economic conditions.

Admittedly, the group features a number of important economies, where indeed investing in reputation has been a conscious policy choice, resorted to after previous dismaying experiences with purely discretionary strategies. If one were inclined to consider the monetary targeting framework still formally prevailing in Germany as a kind of smoke screen raised around the discretionary pursuit of price stability by the central bank, as argued in Section V, then another important country could be added to the list.[28] A further candidate is Italy, where authorities have since 1995 emphasized the need to keep a tight monetary stance regardless of cyclical conditions in order to eliminate deeply-rooted inflationary expectations (Fazio (1996)).

On balance, the evidence suggests that reputational equilibria may be practically unattainable under a fairly large set of circumstances. However, in some, by no means negligible, cases reputation

[25]The official name of Zaïre was changed to Democratic Republic of the Congo on May 17, 1997.

[26]The Bank of Japan, while disclosing one-quarter-ahead projections for broad money since 1978, has never announced a target for any specific monetary aggregate and its implementation of monetary policy has traditionally been "pragmatic" (Swamoto and Ichikawa (1994)).

[27]Throughout the last 50 years, thus including the Bretton Woods period, monetary policy in Lebanon has been discretion based. The civil war disrupted economic activity during the late 1970s and the 1980s brought about high inflation (which never reached the level of some Latin American countries). It is remarkable that the price stabilization over the last 2–3 years has been achieved in the absence of any formal anchor.

[28]In the case of Germany, the decision to emphasize the importance of reputation dates back to the early 1970s, at the time of the conflict between the then President of the Bundesbank, Karl Klasen, and the Minister of Economics, Karl Schiller, which effectively ended with the resignation of the latter. See Goodman (1992).

has played an important role as a credibility-enhancing device. Whether such a role could be sustained in the long run is of course a separate issue, on which the jury is still out.

Institutional Environment and Long-Run Credibility

The above discussion suggests that institutional devices (central bank independence, inflation targeting, IMF-supported programs) can enhance the credibility of low-inflation policies. However, full reliance on institutions runs into a conceptual difficulty. If the inflation bias is ultimately rooted in democratic policymaking, as is widely agreed to be the case (Smith (1992)), how can democratic institutions be expected to enforce sets of rules meant to eradicate the inflation bias itself? This point clearly goes to the heart of the matter: institutional design is often regarded to improve economic performance by raising the costs for policymakers deviating from the socially preferable policy course. But what if there is widespread social consensus on the desirability of the deviation?[29] Should we conclude that monetary institutions work effectively only if they are for all practical purposes redundant?

Advocates of central bank independence often shrug off this type of objection by pointing to the apparently strong correlation between central bank independence and inflation. If the mechanism worked in the past, so the story goes, why should it not be expected to work in the future? But this is clearly a weak counterargument. First, on methodological grounds, it is not obvious that one can infer the desirability of a given arrangement by looking at its impact over a period in which that arrangement was not perceived as operating. A study by Johnson and Siklos (1992), for instance, finds that the reactions of central banks (as measured by changes in interest rates) to shocks to unemployment, inflation, and world interest rates were not closely related to standard measures of central bank independence. If central banks did not regard themselves as being positioned differently depending on their degree of statutory independence, why should the market have re-

---

[29]This consideration casts a shadow on the most recent brand of the time-consistency literature, that on "optimal monetary contracts," pioneered by Walsh (1995) and Persson and Tabellini (1993). On this point, also see McCallum (1996).

acted differently on the basis of the same parameter? Moreover, Posen (1993) is probably right in arguing that a certain degree of public aversion to inflation can be seen as a precondition to the establishment of an independent central bank. We have seen that this has indeed been the case not only in Germany, the country he studies, but also in Italy and New Zealand.

Underscoring the endogenous character of a given institution, however, is not ipso facto evidence of that institution's practical irrelevance. Indeed, that monetary frameworks evolve in response to changing needs has been the key theme throughout the previous sections. Rather, it is a reminder that arrangements meant to credibly constrain governments probably work not so much by raising the cost of breaking their promises as by increasing the perceived benefit of a given policy course or objective, that is, of the promise itself.

This being the case, probably the best yardstick against which to evaluate alternative strategies is the extent to which they can contribute to generate and sustain consensus on the desirability of the social goal they revolve around. In other words, what really matters for the success of monetary reform aiming at price stability is that it be perceived not only as economically meaningful, but also as technically feasible and politically legitimate. One needs only recall the easiness with which the highly autonomous central banks set up in the early 1920s under the auspices of the League of Nations were turned into subjugated governmental agencies as the Great Depression unfolded, to understand that lack of legitimacy can be a serious problem.

From this perspective it may well turn out that the main lesson to be drawn from recent experience is that, given the intrinsically anchorless nature of the fiat standard, creating an ethos of price stability, performing the same function as the ethos of convertibility under the gold standard (Eichengreen (1992)) is really the key issue. It should therefore not come as a surprise that central banks in our days invest considerable amounts of resources in maintaining autonomous and effective research skills, explaining the economic logic underlying their actions (Proske and Penker (1995)), and fostering, even explicitly, a dislike of inflation in the population. An interesting case in point is the recent effort of the Bank of Finland to distribute free publications to the population, even of schooling age, discussing in simple form the costs of inflation and the need for low inflation policies.

V Monetary Anchors

Despite the gradual shift toward discretion illustrated in the previous sections, rule-based frameworks have been very common. This section focuses on these frameworks and on their role as credibility-enhancing devices. It will be argued that the relative diffusion of (multilateral or bilateral) exchange rate pegs—the most common and binding form of rule-based frameworks—may be explained by factors that go beyond the monetary sphere and role of these pegs as credibility-enhancing devices. Cases in which rules were introduced only for monetary purposes—as in examples of monetary targeting—were not only less common, but also involved much milder forms of rules. Thus, the use of strict rules as a device to enhance credibility was less marked than the data surveyed in Section III suggested. Finally, we discuss the role of exchange rate anchors in a world of increased capital mobility.

Past Anchors

Economic literature has repeatedly focused on the alternative between monetary anchors and exchange rate anchors. The information surveyed in Section III suggests that exchange rate anchors have been much more common than monetary anchors, even in recent years. Remarkably, the gradual shift away from exchange rate pegs highlighted in Table 2 coincided only to a very limited extent with an increased use of monetary anchors.

Figure 7 provides further information on the diffusion of monetary targets. As discussed above, monetary announcements characterize both framework 5 and most of the cases included in framework 8. The figure highlights that throughout the past 25 years, monetary targeting has been a relatively uncommon phenomenon.[30] The percentage of countries announc-

ing monetary targets has steadily increased but at a very slow pace: in 1994, only 14 countries were announcing monetary targets. This slow trend increase reflects primarily the behavior of developing countries. In these countries, the discovery of monetary targets is a relatively recent phenomenon, still on the rise, but at a very slow pace and from a very low level. The limited use of monetary targets in developing countries is sometimes not recognized. For example, the literature on stabilization policies in the Southern Cone has frequently contrasted "exchange rate based" stabilizations with "money-based" stabilizations, with Chile in 1974–75, and Argentina in 1976 often quoted as examples of the latter (Kiguel and Liviatan (1994)). However, in neither of these cases were specific money targets or target ranges announced.

In industrial countries, monetary targeting became quite popular soon after the collapse of Bretton Woods and until the early 1980s: at that time, monetary targets were announced in almost one-half of the industrial countries. But since then, the percentage

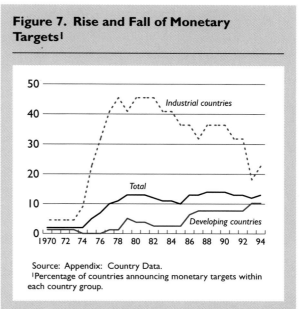

Figure 7. Rise and Fall of Monetary Targets[1]

Source: Appendix: Country Data.
[1]Percentage of countries announcing monetary targets within each country group.

---

[30]A "high inflation" country, Greece, and not Germany (as sometimes argued; see Issing (1995)), was the first to announce annual monetary targets. As argued in Zolotas (1978), money targeting initiated in the early 1950s: "Greece has been a pioneer in this field. . . . The philosophy underlying the setting of a monetary target is that the announcement of and the adherence to the target would combat destabilizing inflationary expectations."

has steadily declined, dropping to less than one-fourth in the mid-1990s. The current diffusion of monetary targets is overestimated by this percentage, as we include in this group all countries announcing monetary aggregates until those aggregates are officially "downgraded" through some official statements. For example, it is well-known that monetary aggregates in the United States—while still announced by the Fed in order to fulfill the requirement of the 1978 Humphrey-Hawkins Act—became de facto less and less relevant throughout the 1980s (Melton and Roley (1990), Bernanke and Mishkin (1992), Crockett (1994), Madigan (1994)). However, we have included the United States in the group of the monetary targeters until February 1993, when Chairman Greenspan in a hearing at the U.S. Senate stated that "M2 has been downgraded as a reliable indicator of financial conditions in the economy, and no single variable has yet been identified to take its place" (Greenspan (1993)). It is also noticeable that broad money targets were, altogether, almost four times more common than narrow money targets. In the sample, there are 148 pairs of year-countries in which broad money was targeted, against only 39 cases in which narrow money was targeted.

The above evidence raises two questions. First, why are monetary targets less common than exchange rate targets? Second, why are monetary targets less common in developing countries? It is worth recalling that internal monetary targeting is quite a common procedure in many central banks of developing countries (Aghevli and others (1979)). What is unusual is the announcement of monetary targets.

One explanation can be found in the literature on optimal control and information variables. Exchange rates might bear a statistically tighter relation with the final targets of monetary policy (say inflation control) than monetary aggregates. Such a feature may be particularly relevant for small developing countries, whose price level is directly affected by exchange rate movements and money velocity may be more unstable, owing to the important role played, in basic financial environments, by monetary assets as a store of value.

There is certainly some truth in this explanation. Figure 8 shows that the volatility of both narrow and broad monies is much higher in developing countries than in industrial countries (in the average of the whole period, by a factor of 1.9 and 2.5, respectively, for narrow and broad money).[31] Moreover, in the average of the whole period, volatility in industrial

countries is higher for narrow money than for broad money. All this is consistent with the evidence that monetary targets are more common in industrial than in developing countries, and that, in countries where monetary targeting is more common, broad money targets are more common than narrow money targets.

After pooling together all available year-framework pairs, we also computed the average volatility of broad money in countries targeting and "nontargeting" broad money: the latter exceeded the former by a factor of 2. Thus, empirical factors do seem to be important in the choice of the nominal anchor.

Yet, the above evidence does not say anything about the relative usefulness as anchor for monetary policy of exchange rates vis-à-vis monetary aggregates. It is somewhat surprising how little attention has been given to exploring systematically this issue. The adoption or rejection of monetary targets is typically premised on studies showing the stability or instability of the money demand equation.[32] But the stability of the exchange rate to price relation has been subject to very limited scrutiny, despite its weak theoretical foundations. The relation is premised on the hypothesis that real exchange rates are constant or predictable, while there is ample evidence that this is not the case. Even assuming that long-run trends in the real exchange rate are relatively predictable, the short-term relation between exchange rates and prices may be unstable (as witnessed by the limited response of inflation to wide exchange rate adjustments in Europe in 1993–94). Moreover, the evidence in Figure 8 does not explain why monetary targets have gradually been abandoned in industrial countries, while they are becoming more common in developing countries. If anything, based on changes in the volatility of money velocity, the opposite could have been expected. All this suggests that other factors may be at play.

A second explanation refers to the "visibility" of exchange rate vis-à-vis monetary anchors: information on exchange rate movements is easily available every day and at virtually no cost, while monetary data may be available only with long lags and at low-frequency intervals (Aghevli, Khan, and Montiel (1991)). This explanation embodies some grain of truth, too, but its importance seems overestimated. Reliable high-frequency monetary statistics are now available in most countries, often with short lags (7–10 days).

---

[31]Following an approach similar to the one in Isard and Rojas-Suarez (1986), and with the same caveats reported there on the limits to this approach, volatility was computed for each country as the standard percentage deviation of velocity around a trend. The figure reported for each year in Figure 8 refers to the simple

average of the volatilities computed for all countries in each group, based on ten-year rolling trends ending in the report year. Note that the number of countries in each group may vary in time as countries shifted in and out of the group of money targeters.

[32]See, with reference to countries rejecting monetary targeting, Bank of Chile (1992); Reserve Bank of New Zealand (1979); Norges Bank (1994); and Central Bank of Iceland (1993). The relation between money demand stability and monetary targeting in the United States is discussed, for example, in Madigan (1994).

We propose here a third explanation, namely, that in a number of cases, exchange rates are introduced and maintained because exchange rate stability is seen as a target in itself, either for economic reasons (minimizing the uncertainty related to foreign trade transactions, which are key to many developing economies) or extra-economic reasons. This hypothesis is supported by two types of evidence.

The first type of evidence refers to the historical origin of multilateral exchange agreements, such as the Bretton Woods system or the ERM. It is by now recognized that the fathers of the Bretton Woods system did not mean it to be a constraint on national monetary policies, but rather a mechanism to avoid "the chaos of the inter-war period," including destabilizing currency speculation, beggar-my-neighbor devaluations, trade restrictions, and exchange controls (Bordo and Eichengreen (1993), Giovannini (1993), Dam (1982)). The ERM was to some extent motivated by the search for monetary stability and "convergence of economic trends" (van Ypersele and Koeune (1984)). But other factors were at play, including a direct dislike for exchange rate uncertainty and strong political goals. Giavazzi and Giovannini (1989) argue that the ERM was the product of the European dislike for exchange rate fluctuations, which they explain with (1) the openness of the European economies; (2) the belief that the floating rates of the 1920s and 1930s were responsible for the collapse of national economies and international trade; and (3) the dependence of postwar European institutions—particularly the common agricultural market—on exchange rate stability.[33] In the same vein, it has been argued that the Monetary Union in Stage III of EMU has primarily a political objective, rather than an economic one.

The second type of evidence concerns the adoption of bilateral exchange rate pegs in developing countries. The empirical evidence in this area indicates that the choice between fixed and flexible exchange rates is influenced primarily by "political and external sector determinants" (Edwards (1995); see also Holden and Holden (1981)). Indeed, based on questionnaires compiled by central banks, Fry, Goodhart, and Almeida (1995) find that, in their sample of 34 developing countries, only 2 countries regarded the exchange rate peg as a nominal anchor.

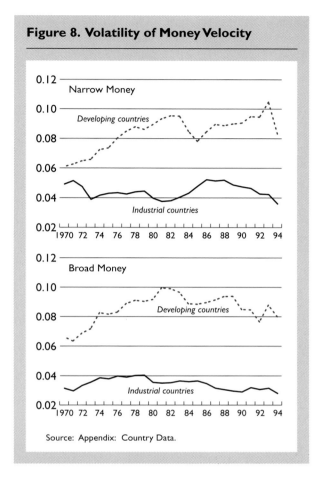

Figure 8. Volatility of Money Velocity

Narrow Money

Developing countries

Industrial countries

Broad Money

Developing countries

Industrial countries

Source: Appendix: Country Data.

The hypothesis that exchange rate pegs are adopted for reasons that go beyond the monetary sphere also explains why monetary targets have remained relatively uncommon. If the exchange rate is a target in itself, it can hardly be replaced by a monetary target. It is therefore interesting to focus on the form taken by actual rules when extramonetary factors were certainly not at play, specifically when monetary targets were used.

The specific forms taken by monetary targeting strongly suggests that this framework often represented a way of giving a rule flavor to policies that remained to a large extent discretionary, although within the constraint of achieving (more or less ambitious) inflation targets.[34] In this respect, two aspects are relevant. A first aspect refers to the extent to which the at-

---

[33]See also Emerson (1979). Governor Baffi, in recalling the negotiations leading to the European Monetary System (EMS), noted that during a difficult meeting with Schmidt "[the German Chancellor] extolled the role of money in the process of political unification, citing the Italian Risorgimento as an example" (Baffi (1989)). Indeed, it is recognized that the EMS was primarily driven by the will of the French and German governments, while it was accepted with less enthusiasm by some central banks, including the Bundesbank (Baffi (1989)) and the Bank of Italy.

---

[34]B. Friedman (1990) surveys the empirical literature addressing the issue of whether the Fed really followed a "money rule," particularly during 1979–82. He concludes that the results "cast doubt on how large a role the monetary target actually played in the Federal Reserve System's decisions on setting interest rates" (pp.1220–21).

tainment of monetary targets was considered binding. In most cases, it was explicitly recognized that monetary targets had to be considered not as binding constraints, but as indicative figures.[35] Even the Bundesbank applied monetary targeting with a feedback mechanism, never refraining "from using new information, for fear of being caught in a credibility dilemma" (Issing (1995)). Indeed, the record of monetary targeting has been quite poor in a number of countries although the monetary targets have frequently been set in terms of, sometimes wide, target ranges (see Griffiths and Wood (1981a), Isard and Rojas-Suarez (1986), Argy, Brennan, and Stevens (1990)).

Second, in almost all cases, monetary (or credit) targets have been announced only for the short run (typically one year ahead) and not over a medium- to long-term horizon. There are two exceptions. First, in the United Kingdom in 1980, as part of the so-called Medium-Term Financial Strategy, monetary targets were announced for four years ahead (Townend (1991)). However, already in 1981, the figure announced for the years beyond the first were downgraded from targets to "illustrative ranges." The second, and more relevant, exception is Switzerland where, as of end-1990, monetary targets have been stated in terms of average annual base growth rate over a 3–5 year period. In this case, however, no specific target was announced for the short run, thus implying that, in principle, the short-term (annual) growth rate of money remained highly uncertain. One can also note that while extreme forms of exchange rate anchors (such as freezing the exchange rate parity for an indefinite period of time) are quite common, correspondingly extreme forms of monetary anchors (such as freezing the quantity of money or its growth rate à la Friedman) are entirely unknown in practice. In many countries, more or less binding constraints have been imposed on base

money growth. An example is given by legislation limiting the growth of central bank credit to the government, which in a few cases has been expressed in terms of maximum contribution to the growth rate of base money (Cottarelli (1993)). But we are not aware of countries in which the total growth rate of base money has ever been legislatively set.

The fact that money targets have been mostly announced for the short term is significant because the recent literature on monetary anchors has stressed that the main purpose of monetary announcements is to affect expectations. As most private sector contracts (including labor contracts) are forward looking, expectations are quite important in shaping price dynamics. But a large share of private sector contracts extends much beyond one year. Moreover, as monetary announcements are typically made once a year, at the moment when the announcement comes, the share of private sector contracts that has already been set may be quite large. Consequently, announcing short-term money targets does not prevent the central bank from surprising the private sector with an unanticipated inflation. Thus, the role of monetary aggregates as expectation anchor was per se limited. Therefore, we submit that the role of monetary targets was mainly to reinforce somewhat the effects of other announcements that monetary policy was turning restrictive and serious about inflation.

Pegs and Capital Mobility

Even though exchange rate pegs have often been introduced for reasons unrelated to monetary control, they have obviously acted as a constraint on monetary policy. In light of this, can they be expected to remain popular in the future as well?

As a matter of fact, Figure 9 shows that the percentage of countries announcing exchange rate pegs (including crawling pegs) has declined over the last 25 years, although the overall trend is more erratic for industrial than for developing countries. Before proceeding, it is useful to recall that the issue here discussed concerns the announcement of exchange rate rules, and not the stability of exchange rates. The latter does not necessarily require the former.

The fall in the popularity of exchange rate pegs is correlated with the gradual removal of capital controls across the world. As shown in Figure 10, the percentage of countries with capital controls dropped from 78 percent in 1978 to 59 percent in 1994. This decline reflects primarily the removal of capital controls in industrial countries,[36] while developing coun-

---

[35]For example, the Humphrey-Hawkins Act indicates that "Nothing in this Act shall be interpreted to require that the objectives and plans with respect to the ranges of growth or diminution of the monetary and credit aggregates disclosed in the reports submitted under this section be achieved if the Board of Governors and the Federal Open Market committee determine that they cannot or should not be achieved because of changing conditions." (Madigan (1994)). Another example is provided by the Report of the Chakravarty Committee (Committee to Review the Working of the Monetary System (1985)), which recommended the introduction of announced monetary targets in India. The Report (paragraph 9.88) stated, "What we have in mind is not mechanistic monetary targeting un-influenced by the impact of developments in the real sector, but what we might characterize as monetary targeting with feedback which enables changes in the targets to be made in the light of emerging trends in output and prices." On this point, see also Rangarajan (1988). In the same vein, the Commission of Inquiry into the Monetary System and Monetary Policy in South Africa recommended that "monetary targeting should be applied in South Africa with a fair measure of flexibility and with a 'low profile'" (South African Reserve Bank (1986)).

---

[36]As of January 1995, Iceland has removed the remaining capital controls, thus completing the process of capital movement liberalization in industrial countries.

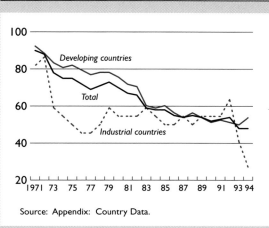

Figure 9. Percentage of Countries with Pegged Exchange Rates

Source: Appendix: Country Data.

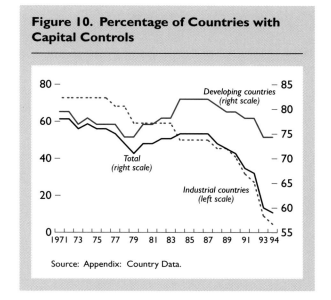

Figure 10. Percentage of Countries with Capital Controls

Source: Appendix: Country Data.

tries have experienced cyclical movements around what appears to be a substantially constant mean. The downward swings in these cyclical movements coincide with favorable macroeconomic conditions. Bartolini and Drazen (1995) have developed a theoretical model of capital controls explaining this feature.

To highlight better the relationship between the exchange rate regime and financial openness, Figure 11 shows the frequency of countries without capital controls within the two groups of "peggers" and "floaters." The figure shows that free capital mobility is clearly more frequent among floaters than among peggers: on the average of the whole period, the percentage of countries with free capital mobility was about 36 percent among floaters, while it was only 23 percent among peggers. The *t* statistics for testing whether the two series reported in Figure 9 have the same average is 9.0, which allows us to reject the null hypothesis at substantially less than the 1 percent level. This means that free capital mobility is more likely to be associated with flexible exchange rates than with pegged exchange rates. The difference between floaters and peggers is much more marked for industrial countries (62 percent against 35 percent) than for developing countries (26 percent against 20 percent), possibly reflecting the lower de facto capital mobility in the latter, even in the absence of capital controls.[37]

The figure also shows that the difference between peggers and floaters in their attitude toward capital controls (the vertical distance between the two lines)

---

[37]Grilli and Milesi-Ferretti (1995) also find that capital controls are more easily found in countries that peg the exchange rate.

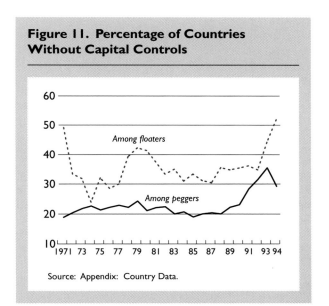

Figure 11. Percentage of Countries Without Capital Controls

Source: Appendix: Country Data.

has not changed substantially throughout the last 25 years: thus, there is no evidence that it is becoming relatively easier for countries with free capital mobility to maintain exchange rate pegs. There is, however, evidence that for both groups of countries, free capital mobility is becoming more common: since the end of the 1980s, both lines in Figure 11 are upward sloping. But this is only a recent phenomenon. During the 1970s and most of the 1980s, the increase in the number of countries without capital controls had been associated with a shift of countries from

Table 8. Joint Distribution of Countries by Exchange Regime and Capital Controls[1]

Framework	1970	1975	1980	1985	1986	1987	1988	1989	1990	1991	1992	1993	1994
Countries with capital controls													
and flexible exchange rates	5	17	17	28	31	32	29	31	32	31	32	29	25
and pegged exchange rates	74	59	56	47	44	43	44	41	39	37	35	31	34
Countries without capital controls													
and flexible exchange rates	5	8	12	14	14	15	15	16	17	17	16	25	27
and pegged exchange rate	16	16	15	11	11	10	12	12	12	15	17	15	14

Source: Appendix: Country Data.
[1]Number of countries in each group.

the group of peggers to the group of floaters, rather than to any significant change of behavior within the two groups.

Further insight can be gained from Table 8, which reports the joint distribution of countries by exchange regime and capital mobility regulations. As the table shows, the increase in the number of countries without capital controls is entirely due to the subgroup of countries adopting flexible exchange rates. There is no trend increase in the number of peggers with free capital mobility (last row)—the number of developing countries with free capital mobility and fixed exchange rates has even *declined* from 13 countries in 1970 to 9 countries in 1994.

More specifically, in 1994, there were only 14 countries with pegged exchange rates and free capital mobility. Five of them adopted very rigid monetary frameworks to bolster the credibility of the peg. These countries include Panama and Kiribati, which do not use domestic currency; and Swaziland, Lesotho, and Argentina, which have established currency boards. The nine remaining countries include (1) five ERM countries that have maintained relatively stable exchange rates even after the widening of the ERM band (Austria, Belgium, France, Ireland, and the Netherlands; Germany is classified as a floater, because it is assumed that it acts as leader of the ERM group); (2) three oil-exporting countries (Bahrain, Oman, and Saudi Arabia); and (3) Uruguay. Thus, even including the wider-bands ERM, maintaining exchange rate pegs, with free capital mobility and in the absence of strong institutional constraints on domestic base money creation, is to be regarded as a very unusual condition.

There is an obvious reason why fixed exchange rates and free capital mobility form an unlikely cou-

ple. A necessary condition for the coexistence of free capital mobility and exchange rate pegs is that the follower country is willing to accept the automatism in monetary policy management implicit in such a rigid framework. For some countries, this automatism may be politically unacceptable (Gros (1988)); it is also suboptimal unless economic shocks are highly correlated across countries. However, the composition of the above sample suggests that the de facto acceptance of automatism may not be sufficient; rather it seems necessary to accept some form of ironclad institutional constraint, such as the adoption of currency boards or monetary unions, going beyond the mere announcement of the exchange rate parity (the relatively good holding of the ERM after the 1992–93 turbulence may indeed be explained by the prospect of the participation in the European Economic and Monetary Union, and the rules related to EMU admission). The number of countries willing to adopt such constraints seems to be limited. The above evidence may be taken as a belated vindication of the Bretton Woods consensus, which pointed to the basic incompatibility of pegged exchange rates with free capital mobility (Marston (1987), Feldstein (1993)).

The above evidence also points at one important effect of increased financial integration: when faced with the choice between maintaining monetary flexibility and pegging the exchange rate, monetary authorities around the world seem to have more and more opted for monetary flexibility. Thus, if the trend toward increased capital mobility continues, exchange rate pegs will possibly lose their role as monetary anchor that they have played in a very large share of countries even after the demise of Bretton Woods.

VI Concluding Remarks

This paper has presented a study of the adaptation of monetary frameworks in the quarter of a century following the demise of Bretton Woods. The absence in this period of recognized worldwide ground rules for the implementation of monetary policy explains the multiplicity of frameworks that have emerged in developing and industrial countries. The paper has, however, shown that, despite differences in specific country experiences and the lack of a grand plan for monetary reform, monetary frameworks did evolve along some clearly discernible patterns, as a response to developments in the macroeconomic environment, economic theory, and popular preferences.

More specifically, the following main conclusions can be drawn from the analysis.

First, the most apparent trend has been the shift toward discretion in the use of monetary policy instruments. This trend was dominated by the gradual abandonment of exchange rate targets both in developing countries (where the process has proceeded gradually and smoothly) and in industrial countries (where the shift has been less smooth). Thus, the "tying one's hands" representation of monetary policy—the adoption of rules to achieve credibility— seems to have become less and less apt to describe actual trends. It has also been shown that the switch toward greater discretion is identifiable not only on average, but also when focusing on countries involved in anti-inflationary efforts.

Second, at the same time, there has been an attempt to conjugate greater flexibility of response with long-run anti-inflationary credibility (or credibility of purpose). This attempt has hinged on three by-now widely shared beliefs, namely that (1) credibility of purpose is indeed the crucial problem to be confronted in the reform process; (2) any policy that aimed at being believed should be based on clear and relatively simple announcements against which to evaluate subsequent policy actions; and (3) some form of delegation is likely to strengthen the credibility of the announced policy path.

Third, the new Weltanschauung, however, has emerged only gradually, and has taken different forms (or strategies). In particular, the paper has highlighted the increasing diffusion of four strategies to achieve credibility: (1) delegation of monetary policy to an independent central bank; (2) increased transparency of the monetary policy process and inflation targeting; (3) greater reliance on an outside source of credibility (for those countries accepting IMF conditionality); and (4) a heavy front-loaded investment in anti-inflationary reputation on the part of monetary authorities. It has also shown that the choice of strategy appears to have been influenced by the institutional environment of the country concerned and by the structure of the economy. In particular, developing countries have mainly chosen the third (and to some extent the first) path. In the industrial world, central bank independence and inflation targeting are instead becoming the dominant mode. At the same time, pure discretion buttressed by reputational forces has successfully been applied only in a very limited (and not increasing) number of countries. Nevertheless, it has been argued that reputation has played an important role in some countries, particularly when coupled with other credibility-enhancing devices. Finally, the paper has argued that the success of the above strategies in the long run ultimately rests on the maintenance of anti-inflationary preferences, which is an ethos of price stability, in the population at large. But, this by no means implies that institutions are irrelevant as institutions and preferences are mutually dependent.

Fourth, as to rule-based frameworks, the paper has shown that domestic anchors (monetary aggregates) have been much less popular than exchange rate anchors, particularly in developing countries. Moreover, they have usually taken milder forms than those adopted when the exchange rate was used as anchor, thus suggesting that monetary targeting often represented a way of giving a rule flavor to policies that remained centered on the flexibility of monetary instruments.

Fifth, in contrast, exchange rate targets were more common and typically took much stronger forms, thus setting correspondingly more binding constraints on monetary policy. At the same time, the paper has argued that the dominance of exchange rate anchors has to be explained also by factors lying outside the monetary domain: exchange rate targets have dominated because they represent targets per se, for either political or psychological reasons. Indeed, the paper suggested that the relative frequency of exchange rate rather than monetary rules confirms that strict adherence to rules, except under extraordinary circumstances, is not an appealing option for monetary authorities unless rules are needed for reasons unrelated to monetary control.

Sixth, the paper argued that one of the factors behind the gradual shift away from exchange rate pegs was the trend increase in capital mobility over the last quarter of a century. If the present trend toward greater capital mobility continues (as we believe will likely be the case, as the process reflects irreversible technological and financial developments), exchange rate pegs are unlikely to come back on stage, except in countries willing to go beyond mere pegging arrangements, toward more extreme forms of monetary policy delegation (such as currency board or monetary unions, as in the case of EMU countries).

Appendix: Country Data

Information from Tables

Information was collected for 100 countries (of which 22 were industrial countries according to the classification published in the IMF's *International Financial Statistics*). The industrial countries in the sample include Australia, Austria, Belgium, Canada, Denmark, Finland, France, Germany, Greece, Iceland, Ireland, Italy, Japan, the Netherlands, New Zealand, Norway, Portugal, Spain, Sweden, Switzerland, the United Kingdom, and the United States. The two remaining industrial countries, which are excluded from the sample, are Luxembourg and San Marino. The information collected concerned four aspects, corresponding to the four rows of the country data tables: (1) announcements involving the existence of domestic anchors for monetary growth; (2) announcements relating to the exchange rate regime; (3) the existence of controls on capital movements; and (4) the existence of IMF-supported programs.

The country tables report annual information on the above aspects for 1970–94. In case of changes during the year, the information refers to the conditions prevailing in most of the year.

Announcements of Domestic Anchors

Included in this group are either institutional arrangements affecting domestic base money creation or the announcement of monetary and inflation targets by the central bank.

More specifically, three institutional arrangements were considered: (1) use of foreign currency as the only legal tender (FC in the tables); (2) participation in a currency union (CU); and (3) currency boards (CB). In none of these arrangements do domestic authorities have discretion on base-money creation. As to monetary targets, for the reasons discussed in the text, only *publicly announced* targets were considered including domestic credit targets (DCT), broad money targets (BMT), narrow money targets (NMT), and base money targets (HMT). Of course, the definitions of narrow or broad money differ somewhat across countries. Targets referring to some subset of base money (e.g., currency in circulation) were classified as base money targets. However, some information on the ex-

istence of targets or projections used internally by central banks are reported in the footnotes of the country tables. Finally, defined as inflation targeting (IT) were the announcements of multiyear targets for inflation, coupled with the introduction of enhanced procedures for monitoring the attainment of those targets.

Exchange Rate Regime

Three exchange rate regimes are distinguished: (1) pegged exchange rate (XXP where XX provides information on the type of peg); (2) crawling peg (XXCP); and (3) flexible exchange rates (FL). More specifically, the tables distinguish between (1) multilateral pegs based on Bretton Woods parities (BWP); (2) multilateral pegs related to the European Common Margin Arrangement (the so-called monetary snake) in operation since March 1972 (ECM); (3) multilateral pegs related to the Exchange Rate Mechanism of the European Monetary System in operation since March 13, 1979 (ERM); (4) trade-weighted pegs (TWP); (5) currency-basket pegs (CBP); and (6) bilateral pegs against Special Drawing Rights (SDP), U.S. dollar (UDP), Indian rupee (IRP), South African rand (SRP), French franc (FFP), ECU (EUP), pounds sterling (LLP), Australian dollar (AUP), and deutsche mark (DMP). In addition, the announcement of a par against gold (arrangement used only in Oman during 1970–72) is indicated with GLP.

The problem of classifying countries across these three categories is notoriously difficult (Quirk (1994)). In group (1) were classified those countries that announced the existence of fixed parities, possibly with a band, with the exception of countries where the parities were regularly and frequently revised, which were classified under (3). All ERM countries, including those participating in the arrangement under a 6 percent band (Portugal, Spain, and the United Kingdom, plus Italy until January 8, 1990) but excluding Germany, were classified in group (1). Germany was classified as floater owing to its role as ERM-leader. On August 3, 1993, the ERM band was raised to 15 percent for all countries. However, ERM countries have continued to be classified in group (1) if in 1994 (that is, after the end of the exchange rate crisis) they maintained, de facto, a "close link" to the central parities, that is, if they maintained the exchange rate within the 2.25 percent band for at least 10 months. The United States was considered among floaters even before the formal closure of the gold window on August 15, 1971, because—as of March 17, 1968—the convertibility of dollar balances had been limited to monetary authorities. Since then, the world monetary system was on a de facto dollar standard (Bordo (1993)). Crawling peggers were characterized by the existence of announced depreciation rates over a certain period of time. All other cases were classified under (3), including cases of pure float in interbank or auction markets, and managed float. Table footnotes provide more detailed information on the specific exchange rate arrangement in place.

Controls on Capital Movements

In the tables, the existence of controls on capital movements is marked by a Y, their absence by an N. The classification follows the information reported under point E.2 (Restrictions on payments for capital transactions) of the table "Summary Features of Exchange and Trade Systems in Member Countries" published in the IMF's *Annual Report on Exchange Arrangements and Exchange Restrictions*. For non-IMF members, information from domestic sources was used.

IMF-Supported Programs

In the tables, Y and N indicate, respectively, the existence or the absence of an IMF-supported program based on the information published in the IMF *Annual Report*. Only programs involving the use of Fund resources and Rights Accumulation Programs (which are programs that countries in arrears with the IMF are requested to undertake before they can borrow again) are considered. However, table footnotes provide information on so-called shadow programs (which are adjustment programs prepared by the IMF under the request of a country, under an enhanced surveillance agreement, but not involving a formal IMF arrangement).

Sources of Information

Most of the information used for the tables was derived from annual reports of central banks. Information was also derived from the reports of the IMF missions, as well as from the following sources:

Argentina: Fasano-Filho (1986), Heymann (1991). *Australia:* Davis and Lewis (1980), Edey and Macfarlane (1991). *Austria:* Hochreiter and Tornquist (1990), Hochreiter and Pech (1991). *Belgium:* Lambert and Jacobs (1991). *Bhutan:* Collyns (1983). *Bolivia:* Sachs (1986). *Botswana:* Bank of Botswana (1985). *Brazil:* Fendt (1981), Cardoso (1991). *Chile:* Edwards and Cox Edwards (1991), Helpman, Leiderman, and Bufman (1994). *Colombia:* Urrutia (1981). *Costa Rica:* Gayle (1986), Guardia Quiros (1993). *Denmark:* De Grauwe and Vanhaverbeke (1990). *Eastern Caribbean Currency Area:* Collyns (1983). *Ecuador:* Ojeda (1985). *Egypt:* Hansen (1991). *Fiji:* Collyns (1983). *Finland:* Aaltonen, Aurikko, and Kontulainen (1994). *France:* Goodman (1992), Icard (1994), de Larosière (1994). *The Gambia:* Hadjimichael, Rumbaugh, and Verreydt (1992). *Ghana:* Amoako (1980), Kapur et al. (1991). *Greece:* Paleologos (1993), Zolotas (1978). *Guinea:* Doré (1986). *Iceland:* Organization for Economic Cooperation and Development (1990). *India:* Rangarajan (1987), Rangarajan (1988), Committee to Review the Working of the Monetary System (1985), Joseph (1992). *Ireland:* Dornbusch (1989), O'Grady Walshe (1991). *Israel:* Bufman, Leiderman, and Sokoler (1994), Helpman, Leiderman, and Bufman (1994). *Italy:* Passacantando (1995). *Jamaica:* Brown (1991). *Japan:* Sawamoto and Ichikawa (1994). *Kenya:* Hazlewood (1979). *Korea:* Aghevli and Márquez-Ruarte (1985). *Lesotho:* Collyns (1983), Lundahl and Petersson (1991). *Malaysia:* See Yan (1991), Hock Pang and Goo Phai (1983), Bank Negara Malaysia (1994). *Mali:* Diarrah (1990). *Mexico:* Ortiz (1991), Weintraub (1981), Helpman, Leiderman, and Bufman (1994). *Morocco:* Nsouli et al. (1995). *Nepal:* Reejal (1986), Sharma (1987). *Netherlands:* Goedhart (1985), Bosman (1984), De Beaufort Wijnholds and Korteweg (1991). *New Zealand:* Blundell-Wignall and Gregory (1990), Reserve Bank of New Zealand (1994). *Nigeria:* Onoh (1980), Okongwu (1986). *Norway:* Gylfason (1990), Brekk (1987), Norges Bank (1994). *Pakistan:* Guisinger (1981), Irfan-ul-Haque (1987), Khan (1993). *Paraguay:* World Bank (1992). *Peru:* Hamann and Paredes (1991), Larrain and Sachs (1991), Cline (1991). *Portugal:* Schmitt (1981). *Singapore:* Bercuson (1995), Wood (1992). *South Africa:* Commission of Inquiry into the Monetary System and Monetary Policy in South Africa (1978). *Spain:* Eguidazu (1978), Escrivá and Malo de Molina (1991). *Sri Lanka:* Athukorala and Jayasuriya (1994). *Swaziland:* Collyns (1983). *Switzerland:* Schiltknecht (1981), Rich (1991). *Thailand:* Bank of Thailand (1992). *Turkey:* Kopits (1987), Celâsun and Rodrik (1987), Ersel and Iskenderoglu (1993). *Uganda:* Sharer et al. (1995). *United Kingdom:* Llewellyn (1982), Townend (1991), Buiter and Miller (1991), Stiehler (1995). *United States:* Tschinkel and Hill (1976), Davis (1977), Friedman (1982), Greenspan (1993), Madigan (1994). *Uruguay:* Ramos (1986), Giorgi (1991), Pascale (1990). *Venezuela:* Crazut (1980), Perez (1994). *West African Monetary Union:* Bhatia (1985). *Zaïre* (Democratic Republic of the Congo): World Bank (1980).

Table A1. Argentina, Australia

	1970	1971	1972	1973	1974	1975	1976	1977	1978	1979	1980	1981
Argentina												
Domestic constraint	—	—	—	—	—	—[1]	—	—	—	DCT[2]	—	—
Exchange rate regime	FL[3]	FL	FL	FL	FL	FL	FL	FL	FL	UDP[4]	UDP	FL
Capital controls	Y	Y	Y	Y	Y	Y	Y	Y	Y	Y	Y	Y
IMF program	N	N	N	N	N	N	N	Y[5]	Y	N	N	N
Australia												
Domestic constraint	—	—	—	—	—[6]	—	BMT[7]	BMT	BMT	BMT	BMT	BMT
Exchange rate regime	BWP	BWP	UDP[8]	UDP	UDP	TWP	TWP	TWP	TWP	TWP	TWP	TWP
Capital controls	Y	Y	Y	Y	Y	Y	Y	Y	Y	Y	Y	Y
IMF program	N	N	N	N	N	N	N	N	N	N	N	N

	1982	1983	1984	1985	1986	1987	1988	1989	1990	1991	1992	1993	1994
Argentina													
Domestic constraint	—	—	—	—	—	—	—	—	—	CB[9]	CB	CB	CB
Exchange rate regime	FL	FL	FL	UDP[10]	FL	FL	FL[11]	FL[12]	FL	UDP[9]	UDP	UDP	UDP
Capital controls	Y	Y	Y	Y	Y	Y	Y	Y	Y	Y	Y	N	N
IMF program	N	Y[13]	N	Y[14]	N	N	Y[15]	Y[16]	Y	Y	Y	Y	Y
Australia													
Domestic constraint	BMT	BMT	BMT[17]	—	—	—	—	—	—	—	—	—	—
Exchange rate regime	TWP	TWP	FL[18]	FL	FL	FL	FL	FL	FL	FL	FL	FL	
Capital controls	Y	Y	N	N	N	N	N	N	N	N	N	N	N
IMF program	N	N	N	N	N	N	N	N	N	N	N	N	N

[1]The April 1975 stabilization is sometimes characterized as "money based" but no money targets were announced.

[2]The central bank announced its commitment to monitor the attainment of the announced targets.

[3]During 1970–78, the exchange rate policy is sometimes characterized as a crawling peg in which the fixed exchange rate was often revised (Fasano-Filho, 1986).

[4]The Tablita stabilization program involving a crawling peg was announced on December 27, 1978 and abandoned at the end of March 1981.

[5]August 6, 1976–August 5, 1977; September 16, 1977–September 15, 1978.

[6]The Bank of Australia started setting unannounced money targets in 1974 (Davis and Lewis, 1980).

[7]First targets announced in March 1976.

[8]The peg was suspended in September 1974. Thereafter, a trade-weighted peg was introduced; a variable link was introduced at end-November 1976.

[9]The "Convertibilidad Law" of March 27, 1991 fixed the exchange rate of the austral and introduced a currency board arrangement for the central bank, severely limiting the scope for domestic base money creation.

[10]The Austral stabilization plan of June 1985 fixed the exchange rate; in April 1986, the government announced that the rate would be periodically adjusted; in August 1986, it announced a policy of adjustment at declined rates.

[11]The primavera program of August 1988 introduced a new foreign exchange system in which a "free" exchange rate used for imports and financial transactions would float, and the pegged official rates would be subject to step-wise adjustments.

[12]The stabilization plan of July 1989 involved a freeze of the official exchange rate. The plan was abandoned in December 1989 when the exchange rate was floated.

[13]January 24, 1983–April 23, 1984.

[14]December 28, 1984–March 27, 1986.

[15]July 23, 1987–September 30, 1990.

[16]May 31, 1989–May 30, 1990; November 10, 1989–March 31, 1991; July 29, 1991–June 30, 1992; and March 31, 1992–March 30, 1995.

[17]Monetary targeting is abandoned in January 1985 (Edey and Mcfarlane, 1991).

[18]The exchange rate was floated as of December 1983.

Table A2. Austria, Bahamas

	1970	1971	1972	1973	1974	1975	1976	1977	1978	1979	1980	1981
Austria												
Domestic constraint	—	—	—	—	—	—	—	—	—	—	—	—
Exchange rate regime	BWP	BWP[1]	CBP	CBP	CBP	CBP	CBP	CBP	CBP	CBP	CBP	DMP
Capital controls	Y	Y	Y	Y	Y	Y	Y	Y	Y	Y	Y	Y
IMF program	N	N	N	N	N	N	N	N	N	N	N	N
Bahamas												
Domestic constraint	—	—	—	—	—	—	—	—	—	—	—	—
Exchange rate regime	UDP	UDP	UDP	UDP	UDP	UDP	UDP	UDP	UDP	UDP	UDP	UDP
Capital controls	Y	Y	Y	Y	Y	Y	Y	Y	Y	Y	Y	Y
IMF program	N	N	N	N	N	N	N	N	N	N	N	N

	1982	1983	1984	1985	1986	1987	1988	1989	1990	1991	1992	1993	1994
Austria													
Domestic constraint	—	—	—	—	—	—	—	—	—	—	—	—	—
Exchange rate regime	DMP	DMP	DMP	DMP	DMP	DMP	DMP	DMP	DMP	DMP	DMP	DMP	DMP
Capital controls	Y	Y	Y	Y	Y	Y	Y	Y	N	N	N	N	
IMF program	N	N	N	N	N	N	N	N	N	N	N	N	N
Bahamas													
Domestic constraint	—	—	—	—	—	—	—	—	—	—	—	—	—
Exchange rate regime	UDP	UDP	UDP	UDP	UDP	UDP	UDP	UDP	UDP	UDP	UDP	UDP	UDP
Capital controls	Y	Y	Y	Y	Y	Y	Y	Y	Y	Y	Y	Y	Y
IMF program	N	N	N	N	N	N	N	N	N	N	N	N	N

[1]After August 1971, the shilling was pegged to a currency basket including initially six currencies. Over time, the weaker currencies were gradually eliminated from the basket and by 1981, a DM peg had (informally) been established (Hochreiter and Tornquist (1990)).

Table A3. Bahrain, Barbados

	1970	1971	1972	1973	1974	1975	1976	1977	1978	1979	1980	1981
Bahrain												
Domestic constraint	—	—	—	—	—	—	—	—	—	—	—	—
Exchange rate regime	BWP	BWP	BWP	UDP	UDP	UDP	UDP	UDP	UDP[1]	UDP	UDP	UDP
Capital controls	N	N	N	N	N	N	N	N	N	N	N	N
IMF program	N	N	N	N	N	N	N	N	N	N	N	N
Barbados												
Domestic constraint	CU	CU	CU	CU	—[2]	—	—	—	—	—	—	—
Exchange rate regime	UDP	UDP	UDP	UDP	LLP	LLP	UDP[3]	UDP	UDP	UDP	UDP	UDP
Capital controls	Y	Y	Y	Y	Y	Y	Y	Y	Y	Y	Y	Y
IMF program	N	N	N	N	N	N	N	N	N	N	N	N

	1982	1983	1984	1985	1986	1987	1988	1989	1990	1991	1992	1993	1994
Bahrain													
Domestic constraint	—	—	—	—	—	—	—	—	—	—	—	—	—
Exchange rate regime	UDP	UDP	UDP	UDP	UDP	UDP	UDP	UDP	UDP	UDP	UDP	UDP	UDP
Capital controls	N	N	N	N	N	N	N	N	N	N	N	N	N
IMF program	N	N	N	N	N	N	N	N	N	N	N	N	N
Barbados													
Domestic constraint	—	—	—	—	—	—	—	—	—	—	—	—	—
Exchange rate regime	UDP	UDP	UDP	UDP	UDP	UDP	UDP	UDP	UDP	UDP	UDP	UDP	UDP
Capital controls	Y	Y	Y	Y	Y	Y	Y	Y	Y	Y	Y	Y	Y
IMF program	N	Y[4]	N	N	N	N	N	N	N	N	Y[5]	N	N

[1]Since 1978, the dinar is officially pegged to the SDR; in practice, however, the dinar/dollar exchange rate has remained fixed since December 1980.

[2]On December 3, 1973, the Central Bank of Barbados, which had been set up in May 1972, started issuing its own currency. At the same time, Barbados withdrew from the Eastern Caribbean Currency Authority.

[3]As of July 5, 1975.

[4]October 1, 1982–May 31, 1984.

[5]February 7, 1992–May 31, 1993.

Table A4. Belgium, Benin

	1970	1971	1972	1973	1974	1975	1976	1977	1978	1979	1980	1981
Belgium												
Domestic constraint	—	—	—	—	—	—	—	—	—	—	—	—
Exchange rate regime	BWP	BWP	ECM	ECM	ECM	ECM	ECM	ECM	ECM	ERM	ERM	ERM
Capital controls	N	N	N	N	N	N	N	N	N	N	N	N
IMF program	N	N	N	N	N	N	N	N	N	N	N	N
Benin												
Domestic constraint	CU	CU	CU	CU	CU	CU	CU	CU	CU	CU	CU	CU
Exchange rate regime	FFP	FFP	FFP	FFP	FFP	FFP	FFP	FFP	FFP	FFP	FFP	FFP
Capital controls	Y	Y	Y	Y	Y	Y	Y	Y	Y	Y	Y	Y
IMF program	N	N	N	N	N	N	N	N	N	N	N	N

	1982	1983	1984	1985	1986	1987	1988	1989	1990	1991	1992	1993	1994
Belgium													
Domestic constraint	—	—	—	—	—	—	—	—	—	—	—	—	—
Exchange rate regime	ERM	ERM	ERM	ERM	ERM	ERM	ERM	ERM	ERM	ERM	ERM	ERM	ERM
Capital controls	N	N	N	N	N	N	N	N	N	N	N	N	N
IMF program	N	N	N	N	N	N	N	N	N	N	N	N	N
Benin													
Domestic constraint	CU	CU	CU	CU	CU	CU	CU	CU	CU	CU	CU	CU	CU
Exchange rate regime	FFP	FFP	FFP	FFP	FFP	FFP	FFP	FFP	FFP	FFP	FFP	FFP	FFP
Capital controls	Y	Y	Y	Y	Y	Y	Y	Y	Y	Y	Y	Y	Y
IMF program	N	N	N	N	N	N	N	Y[1]	Y	Y	Y	Y	Y

[1]June 16, 1989–June 15, 1992; January 25, 1993–January 24, 1996.

Table A5. Bhutan, Bolivia

	1970	1971	1972	1973	1974	1975	1976	1977	1978	1979	1980	1981
Bhutan												
Domestic constraint	FC	FC	FC	FC[1]	—	—	—	—	—	—	—	—
Exchange rate regime	IRP	IRP	IRP	IRP	IRP	IRP	IRP	IRP	IRP	IRP	IRP	IRP
Capital controls	Y[2]	Y	Y	Y	Y	Y	Y	Y	Y	Y	Y	Y
IMF program	N	N	N	N	N	N	N	N	N	N	N	N
Bolivia												
Domestic constraint	—	—	—	—	—	—	—	—	—	—	—	—
Exchange rate regime	BWP	BWP	UDP	UDP	UDP	UDP	UDP	UDP	UDP	UDP	UDP	UDP[3]
Capital controls	N	N	N	N	N	N	N	N	N	N	Y	Y
IMF program	N	N	N	Y[4]	N	N	N	N	N	N	Y[5]	N

	1982	1983	1984	1985	1986	1987	1988	1989	1990	1991	1992	1993	1994
Bhutan													
Domestic constraint	—	—	—	—	—	—	—	—	—	—	—	—	—
Exchange rate regime	IRP	IRP	IRP	IRP	IRP	IRP	IRP	IRP	IRP	IRP	IRP	IRP	IRP
Capital controls	Y	Y	Y	Y	Y	Y	Y	Y	Y	Y	Y	Y	Y
IMF program	N	N	N	N	N	N	N	N	N	N	N	N	N
Bolivia													
Domestic constraint	—	—	—	—	—	—	—	—	—	—	—	—	—
Exchange rate regime	UDP	UDP	UDP	FL[6]	FL	FL	FL	FL	FL	FL	FL	FL	FL
Capital controls	Y	Y	Y	Y	N	N	N	N	N	N	N	N	N
IMF program	N	N	N	N	Y[7]	Y	Y	Y	Y	Y	Y	Y	Y

[1]Before 1974, the Indian rupee was used as domestic currency. The Bhutanese ngultrum was introduced only in 1974. The Royal Monetary Authority of Bhutan was established only in 1983.

[2]Large capital movements with India must be approved by the Ministry of Finance.

[3]Between 1981 and 1985, the pegged exchange rate that had remained stable in the 1970s was repeatedly devalued.

[4]January 17, 1973–January 16, 1974.

[5]February 1, 1980–January 31, 1981.

[6]With the August 29, 1985 stabilization package, the exchange rate was floated.

[7]June 19, 1986–June 18, 1987; December 15, 1986–December 14, 1989; July 27, 1988–March 31, 1994; December 19, 1994–December 18, 1997.

Table A6. Botswana, Brazil

	1970	1971	1972	1973	1974	1975	1976	1977	1978	1979	1980	1981
Botswana												
Domestic constraint	FC	FC	FC	FC	FC	FC	FC	—	—	—	—	—
Exchange rate regime	SRP[1]	SRP	SRP	SRP	SRP	SRP	SRP	UDP[2]	UDP	UDP	CBP[3]	CBP
Capital controls	Y	Y	Y	Y	Y	Y	Y	Y	Y	Y	Y	Y
IMF program	—	—	—	—	—	—	—	—	—	—	—	—
Brazil												
Domestic constraint	—	—	—	—	—	—	—	BMT	—	—	—	—
Exchange rate regime	FL[4]	FL	FL	FL	FL	FL	FL	FL	FL	FL	UDCP[5]	FL
Capital controls	Y	Y	Y	Y	Y	Y	Y	Y	Y	Y	Y	Y
IMF program	Y[6]	Y	Y	N	N	N	N	N	N	N	N	N

	1982	1983	1984	1985	1986	1987	1988	1989	1990	1991	1992	1993	1994
Botswana													
Domestic constraint	—	—	—	—	—	—	—	—	—	—	—	—	—
Exchange rate regime	CBP	CBP	CBP	CBP	CBP	CBP	CBP	CBP	CBP	CBP	CBP	CBP	CBP
Capital controls	Y	Y	Y	Y	Y	Y	Y	Y	Y	Y	Y	Y	Y
IMF program	—	—	—	—	—	—	—	—	—	—	—	—	—
Brazil													
Domestic constraint	—	—	—	—	—	—	—	—[7]	—	—	—	—	—
Exchange rate regime	FL	FL	FL	FL	UDP[8]	FL	FL	FL[9]	FL[10]	FL	FL	FL	FL
Capital controls	Y	Y	Y	Y	Y	Y	Y	Y	Y	Y	Y	Y	Y
IMF program	N	Y[11]	Y	Y	N	N	N	Y[12]	N	N	Y[13]	Y	N

[1]Until August 26, 1976, when the pula was introduced, the South African rand was used as legal tender.

[2]The pula was pegged to the U.S. dollar from August 26, 1976 (when it was introduced) to May 27, 1980.

[3]Since June 2, 1980, the pula has been formally pegged to a basket of currencies; the parities are, however, revised from time to time, albeit not frequently, in light of domestic policy considerations.

[4]As of August 1968, the exchange rate followed a crawling peg in which the exchange rate was adjusted at the discretion of the authorities; this system lasted for most of the period here considered (with the exceptions reported in the table). In March 1990, the exchange rate was formally floated. In June 1994, in connection with the real stabilization plan, an exchange rate floor was introduced. On March 6, 1995, the authorities switched to explicit and adjustable exchange rate bands.

[5]The exchange rate depreciation was targeted to be 40 percent in 1980 (actual depreciation was 54 percent).

[6]April 29, 1969–April 28, 1970; February 2, 1970–February 3, 1972; March 3, 1972–March 2, 1973.

[7]The March 1990 stabilization plan involved a drastic reduction in liquidity through a temporary blocking of about two-thirds of M4; however, no target was announced for monetary growth.

[8]Between February 1986 and late 1986, as part of the cruzado stabilization plan, the exchange rate was pegged.

[9]As part of the summer plan of January 1989, the exchange rate was pegged; but the peg lasted only a few months.

[10]The exchange rate was floated as of March 1990, although intervention in the foreign exchange market continued.

[11]March 1, 1983–February 28, 1986.

[12]August 23, 1988–February 28, 1990.

[13]January 29, 1992–August 31, 1993.

Table A7. Burkina Faso, Cameroon

	1970	1971	1972	1973	1974	1975	1976	1977	1978	1979	1980	1981
Burkina Faso												
Domestic constraint	CU	CU	CU	CU	CU	CU	CU	CU	CU	CU	CU	CU
Exchange rate regime	FFP	FFP	FFP	FFP	FFP	FFP	FFP	FFP	FFP	FFP	FFP	FFP
Capital controls	Y	Y	Y	Y	Y	Y	Y	Y	Y	Y	Y	Y
IMF program	N	N	N	N	N	N	N	N	N	N	N	N
Cameroon												
Domestic constraint	CU	CU	CU	CU	CU	CU	CU	CU	CU	CU	CU	CU
Exchange rate regime	FFP	FFP	FFP	FFP	FFP	FFP	FFP	FFP	FFP	FFP	FFP	FFP
Capital controls	Y	Y	Y	Y	Y	Y	Y	Y	Y	Y	Y	Y
IMF program	N	N	N	N	N	N	N	N	N	N	N	N

	1982	1983	1984	1985	1986	1987	1988	1989	1990	1991	1992	1993	1994
Burkina Faso													
Domestic constraint	CU	CU	CU	CU	CU	CU	CU	CU	CU	CU	CU	CU	CU
Exchange rate regime	FFP	FFP	FFP	FFP	FFP	FFP	FFP	FFP	FFP	FFP	FFP	FFP	FFP
Capital controls	Y	Y	Y	Y	Y	Y	Y	Y	Y	Y	Y	Y	Y
IMF program	N	N	N	N	N	N	N	N	N	Y[1]	Y	Y	Y
Cameroon													
Domestic constraint	CU	CU	CU	CU	CU	CU	CU	CU	CU	CU	CU	CU	CU
Exchange rate regime	FFP	FFP	FFP	FFP	FFP	FFP	FFP	FFP	FFP	FFP	FFP	FFP	FFP
Capital controls	Y	Y	Y	Y	Y	Y	Y	Y	Y	Y	Y	Y	Y
IMF program	N	N	N	N	N	N	N	Y[2]	N	N	N	N	Y[3]

[1]March 13, 1991–March 12, 1994; March 31, 1993–March 30, 1996.
[2]September. 19, 1988–March 31, 1990.
[3]March 14, 1994–September 13, 1995.

Table A8. CAMU (Central African Monetary Union), Canada

	1970	1971	1972	1973	1974	1975	1976	1977	1978	1979	1980	1981
CAMU[1]												
Domestic constraint	—	—	—	—	—	—	—	—	—	—	—	—
Exchange rate regime	FFP	FFP	FFP	FFP	FFP	FFP	FFP	FFP	FFP	FFP	FFP	FFP
Capital controls	Y	Y	Y	Y	Y	Y	Y	Y	Y	Y	Y	Y
IMF program	N	N	N	N	N	N	N	N	N	N	N	N
Canada												
Domestic constraint	—	—	—	—	—	—	NMT[2]	NMT	NMT	NMT	NMT	NMT
Exchange rate regime	FL[3]	FL	FL	FL	FL	FL	FL	FL	FL[4]	FL	FL	FL
Capital controls	N	N	N	N	N	N	N	N	N	N	N	N
IMF program	N	N	N	N	N	N	N	N	N	N	N	N

	1982	1983	1984	1985	1986	1987	1988	1989	1990	1991	1992	1993	1994
CAMU[1]													
Domestic constraint	—	—	—	—	—	—	—	—	—	—	—[5]	—	—
Exchange rate regime	FFP	FFP	FFP	FFP	FFP	FFP	FFP	FFP	FFP	FFP	FFP	FFP	FFP
Capital controls	Y	Y	Y	Y	Y	Y	Y	Y	Y	Y	Y	Y	Y
IMF program	N	N	N	N	N	N	N	N	N	N	N	N	N
Canada													
Domestic constraint	NMT[6]	—	—	—	—	—	—	—	—	IT[7]	IT	IT	IT
Exchange rate regime	FL	FL	FL	FL	FL	FL	FL	FL	FL	FL	FL	FL	FL
Capital controls	N	N	N	N	N	N	N	N	N	N	N	N	N
IMF program	N	N	N	N	N	N	N	N	N	N	N	N	N

[1]Cameroon, Central African Republic, Chad, Republic of Congo, Equatorial Guinea, and Gabon.

[2]Announced in November 1975.

[3]The Canadian dollar was floated in May 1970.

4During 1978–83, there was a strong attempt to stabilize the exchange rate vis-à-vis the U.S. dollar (see, for example, Bernanke and Mishkin (1992)).

[5]As of 1992, the BEAC (Bank of Central African States—the Central Bank of the CAMU) began setting annual targets for monetary aggregates; these targets, however, are not publicly announced.

[6]Target dropped in November 1982.

[7]Announced in February 1991 by the government and the Bank of Canada.

Table A9. Central African Republic, Chad

	1970	1971	1972	1973	1974	1975	1976	1977	1978	1979	1980	1981
Central African Republic												
Domestic constraint	CU	CU	CU	CU	CU	CU	CU	CU	CU	CU	CU	CU
Exchange rate regime	FFP	FFP	FFP	FFP	FFP	FFP	FFP	FFP	FFP	FFP	FFP	FFP
Capital controls	Y	Y	Y	Y	Y	Y	Y	Y	Y	Y	Y	Y
IMF program	N	N	N	N	N	N	N	N	N	N	Y[1]	Y
Chad												
Domestic constraint	CU	CU	CU	CU	CU	CU	CU	CU	CU	CU	CU	CU
Exchange rate regime	FFR	FFR	FFR	FFR	FFR	FFR	FFR	FFR	FFR	FFR	FFR	FFR
Capital controls	Y	Y	Y	Y	Y	Y	Y	Y	Y	Y	Y	Y
IMF program	N	N	N	N	N	N	N	N	N	N	N	N

	1982	1983	1984	1985	1986	1987	1988	1989	1990	1991	1992	1993	1994
Central African Republic													
Domestic constraint	CU	CU	CU	CU	CU	CU	CU	CU	CU	CU	CU	CU	CU
Exchange rate regime	FFP	FFP	FFP	FFP	FFP	FFP	FFP	FFP	FFP	FFP	FFP	FFP	FFP
Capital controls	Y	Y	Y	Y	Y	Y	Y	Y	Y	Y	Y	Y	Y
IMF program	N	Y[2]	Y	Y	Y	Y	Y	Y	N	N	N	N	Y[3]
Chad													
Domestic constraint	CU	CU	CU	CU	CU	CU	CU	CU	CU	CU	CU	CU	CU
Exchange rate regime	FFR	FFR	FFR	FFR	FFR	FFR	FFR	FFR	FFR	FFR	FFR	FFR	FFR
Capital controls	Y	Y	Y	Y	Y	Y	Y	Y	Y	Y	Y	Y	Y
IMF program	N	N	N	N	N	N	Y[4]	Y	Y	N	N	N	Y[5]

[1]February 15, 1980–February 15, 1981; April 10, 1981–December 31, 1981.
[2]April 22, 1983–April 21, 1984; July 6, 1984–July 5, 1985; September 23, 1985–March 27, 1987; June 1, 1987–May 31, 1990.
[3]March 28, 1994–March 27, 1995.
[4]October 30, 1987–October 29, 1990.
[5]March 23, 1994–March 22, 1995.

Table A10. Chile, Colombia

	1970	1971	1972	1973	1974	1975	1976	1977	1978	1979	1980	1981
Chile												
Domestic constraint	—	—	—	—	—	—[1]	—	—	—	—	—	—
Exchange rate regime	BWP	BWP	BWP	FL[2]	FL	FL	FL	FL	UDP[3]	UDP	UDP	UDP
Capital controls	Y	Y	Y	Y	Y	Y	Y	Y	Y	Y	Y	Y
IMF program	N[4]	N	N	N	Y[5]	Y[6]	N	N	N	N	N	N
Colombia												
Domestic constraint	—	—	—	—	—	—	—	—	—	—	—	—
Exchange rate regime	BWP	BWP	FL[7]	FL	FL	FL	FL	FL	FL	FL	FL	FL
Capital controls	Y	Y	Y	Y	Y	Y	Y	Y	Y	Y	Y	Y
IMF program	Y[8]	Y	Y	Y	N	N	N	N	N	N	N	N

	1982	1983	1984	1985	1986	1987	1988	1989	1990	1991	1992	1993	1994
Chile													
Domestic constraint	—	—	—	—	—	—	—	—	—	—	—	—	—
Exchange rate regime	UDP	FL	FL	FL	UDP[9]	UDP	UDP	UDP	UDP	UDP	UDP	CBP	CBP
Capital controls	Y	Y	Y	Y	Y	Y	Y	Y	Y	Y	Y	Y	Y
IMF program	N	Y[10]	Y	N	Y[11]	Y	Y	Y	Y[12]	N	N	N	N
Colombia													
Domestic constraint	—	—	—	—	—	—	—	—	—	—	—	NMT[13]	NMT
Exchange rate regime	FL	FL	FL	FL	FL	FL	FL	FL	FL	FL	FL	FL	UDP[14]
Capital controls	Y	Y	Y	Y	Y	Y	Y	Y	Y	Y	Y	Y	Y
IMF program	N	N	N	N	N	N	N	N	N	N	N	N	N

[1]In 1975–77, a stabilization based on tight monetary policy was attempted; money targets, however, were not announced.

[2]In October 1973, a crawling peg was adopted; the exchange rate was periodically revised but the depreciation schedule was not announced; between July 1977 and February 1978, a daily depreciation schedule was announced at the beginning of each month.

[3]Announced in February 1978; the predetermined crawling peg (tablita) was replaced in June 1979 by a fixed exchange rate, which was abandoned in the third quarter of 1982.

[4]April 19, 1969–April 18, 1970.

[5]January 30, 1974–January 28, 1975.

[6]March 19, 1975–March 18, 1976.

[7]The exchange rate followed a crawling peg in which the rate of crawl was not announced.

[8]April 21, 1970–April 20, 1972; May 1, 1972–April 30, 1973; June 6, 1973–June 5, 1974.

[9]Between January 1986 and April 1988, a 2 percent band was in place; the band was 3 percent during May 1988–May 1989; the band was 5 percent during June 1989–December 1991; the band was 10 percent during January–June 1992; the basket was introduced in July 1992.

[10]January 10, 1983–January 9, 1985.

[11]August 15, 1985–August 14, 1989.

[12]November 8, 1989–November 7, 1990.

[13]Targets for narrow money were announced for the year 1993 in a letter from the Banco de la República to the finance minister on November 12, 1992. The letter was published in the same month in the monthly bulletin of the central bank.

[14]In early 1994, a band around an average depreciation rate vis-à-vis the U.S. dollar was announced.

Table A11. Republic of Congo, Costa Rica

	1970	1971	1972	1973	1974	1975	1976	1977	1978	1979	1980	1981
Congo, Republic of												
Domestic constraint	CU	CU	CU	CU	CU	CU	CU	CU	CU	CU	CU	CU
Exchange rate regime	FFR	FFR	FFR	FFR	FFR	FFR	FFR	FFR	FFR	FFR	FFR	FFR
Capital controls	Y	Y	Y	Y	Y	Y	Y	Y	Y	Y	Y	Y
IMF program	N	N	N	N	N	N	N	Y[1]	N	Y[2]	N	N
Costa Rica												
Domestic constraint	—	—	—	—	—	—	—	—	—	—[3]	—	—
Exchange rate regime	BWP	BWP	UDP	UDP	UDP	UDP	UDP	UDP	UDP	UDP	UDP	UDP
Capital controls	N	N	N	N	Y	Y	Y	Y	Y	Y	N	N
IMF program	N	N	N	N	N	N	N	Y[4]	N	N	Y[5]	Y

	1982	1983	1984	1985	1986	1987	1988	1989	1990	1991	1992	1993	1994
Congo, Republic of													
Domestic constraint	CU	CU	CU	CU	CU	CU	CU	CU	CU	CU	CU	CU	CU
Exchange rate regime	FFR	FFR	FFR	FFR	FFR	FFR	FFR	FFR	FFR	FFR	FFR	FFR	FFR
Capital controls	Y	Y	Y	Y	Y	Y	Y	Y	Y	Y	Y	Y	Y
IMF program	N	N	N	N	N	Y[6]	Y	N	N	Y[7]	N	N	Y[8]
Costa Rica													
Domestic constraint	—	—	—	—	—	—	—	—	—	—	—	—	—
Exchange rate regime	FL[9]	FL	FL	FL	FL	FL	FL	FL	FL	FL	FL	FL	FL
Capital controls	Y	Y	Y	Y	Y	Y	Y	Y	Y	Y	Y	Y	Y
IMF program	Y	Y	Y	Y	N	N	Y[10]	Y	N	Y[11]	N	Y[12]	N

[1]January 1, 1977–December 31, 1977.

[2]April 25, 1979–April 24, 1980.

[3]During the 1980s, and even before, the central bank prepared an annual credit program used to set ceilings on bank credit including "targets" for the main money and credit aggregates. These targets, however, were not announced.

[4]July 23, 1976–July 22, 1977.

[5]March 12, 1980–March 11, 1982; June 17, 1981–June 11, 1984; March 13, 1985–April 12, 1986.

[6]August 29, 1986–August 28, 1988.

[7]August 27, 1990–May 26, 1992.

[8]May 27, 1994–May 26, 1995.

[9]The exchange rate of the colon against that of the U.S. dollar had been legally set; on December 3, 1981, parliament devalued the colon but the devaluation was not considered sufficient by the central bank, which started a free market in parallel with the official one, as allowed by the central bank law. A period of multiple exchange rates and minidevaluations began; the exchange rates were unified on November 11, 1983, but the crawling peg continued until March 1991, when the colon was floated.

[10]October 28, 1987–March 31, 1982.

[11]April 8, 1991–April 7, 1992.

[12]April 19, 1993–February 18, 1994.

Table A12. Cyprus, Denmark

	1970	1971	1972	1973	1974	1975	1976	1977	1978	1979	1980	1981
Cyprus												
Domestic constraint[1]	—	—	—	—	—	—	—	—	—	—	—	—
Exchange rate regime	LLP	LLP	LLP	LLP	LLP	LLP	TWP[2]	TWP	TWP	TWP	TWP	TWP
Capital controls	Y	Y	Y	Y	Y	Y	Y	Y	Y	Y	Y	Y
IMF program	N	N	N	N	N	N	N	N	N	N	N	Y[3]
Denmark												
Domestic constraint	—	—	—	—	—	—	—	—	—	—	—	—
Exchange rate regime	BWP	BWP	ECM	ECM	ECM	ECM	ECM	ECM	ECM	ERM	ERM	ERM
Capital controls	Y	Y	Y	Y	Y	Y	Y	Y	Y	Y	Y	Y
IMF program	N	N	N	N	N	N	N	N	N	N	N	N

	1982	1983	1984	1985	1986	1987	1988	1989	1990	1991	1992	1993	1994
Cyprus													
Domestic constraint[1]	—	—	—	—	—	—	—	—	—	—	—	—	—
Exchange rate regime	TWP	TWP	TWP	TWP	TWP	TWP	TWP	TWP	TWP	TWP	EUP[4]	EUP	EUP
Capital controls	Y	Y	Y	Y	Y	Y	Y	Y	Y	Y	Y	Y	Y
IMF program	N	N	N	N	N	N	N	N	N	N	N	N	N
Denmark													
Domestic constraint	—	—	—	—	—	—	—	—	—	—	—	—	—
Exchange rate regime	ERM[5]	ERM	ERM	ERM	ERM	ERM	ERM	ERM	ERM	ERM	ERM	ERM	ERM
Capital controls	Y	Y	Y	Y	Y	Y	N	N	N	N	N	N	N
IMF program	N	N	N	N	N	N	N	N	N	N	N	N	N

[1]Targets are not announced to the public; however, the Central Bank of Cyprus provides information to banks on the target for bank credit to the private sector.

[2]June 1976.

[3]July 16, 1980–July 15, 1981.

[4]June 1992.

[5]The Danish stabilization program of 1982 did not involve any formal change in the policy framework but, rather, the decision to stop the policy of creeping devaluations and to peg the krone to the DM.

Table A13. Dominican Republic, Eastern Caribbean Currency Area

	1970	1971	1972	1973	1974	1975	1976	1977	1978	1979	1980	1981
Dominican Republic												
Domestic constraint	—	—	—	—	—	—	—	—	—	—	—	—
Exchange rate regime	UDP	UDP	UDP	UDP	UDP	UDP	UDP	UDP	UDP	UDP	UDP	UDP
Capital controls	Y	Y	Y	Y	Y	Y	Y	Y	Y	Y	Y	Y
IMF program	N	N	N	N	N	N	N	N	N	N	N	N
Eastern Caribbean Currency Area[1]												
Domestic constraint	—	—	—	—	—	—	—	—	—	—	—	—
Exchange rate regime	UDP	UDP	UDP	UDP	UDP	UDP	UDP	UDP	UDP	UDP	UDP	UDP
Capital controls	I	I	I	I	I	I	I	I	I	I	I	I
IMF program	—	—	—	—	—	—	—	—	—	—	—	—

	1982	1983	1984	1985	1986	1987	1988	1989	1990	1991	1992	1993	1994
Dominican Republic													
Domestic constraint	—	—	—	—	—	—	—	—	—	—	—	—	—
Exchange rate regime	UDP	UDP	UDP	FL[2]	FL	FL	FL	FL	FL	FL	FL	FL	FL
Capital controls	Y	Y	Y	Y	Y	Y	Y	Y	Y	Y	Y	Y	Y
IMF program	N	Y[3]	Y	Y	N	N	N	N	N	N	Y[4]	Y	N
Eastern Caribbean Currency Area[1]													
Domestic constraint	—	—	—	—	—	—	—	—	—	—	—	—	—
Exchange rate regime	UDP	UDP	UDP	UDP	UDP	UDP	UDP	UDP	UDP	UDP	UDP	UDP	UDP
Capital controls	I	I	I	I	I	I	I	I	I	I	I	I	I
IMF program	—	—	—	—	—	—	—	—	—	—	—	—	—

[1]The Eastern Caribbean Currency Area includes seven countries: Antigua and Barbuda, Dominica, Grenada, Montserrat, St. Kitts and Nevis, St. Lucia, and St. Vincent. Barbados withdrew from this arrangement in 1974.

[2]In January 1985, the exchange rate was floated; in the following years (e.g., in 1990), there were attempts to reintroduce a dollar peg, including through multiple fixed exchange rates.

[3]January 27, 1983–January 20, 1986; April 15, 1985–April 14, 1986.

[4]August 28, 1991–March 27, 1993; July 9, 1993–March 28, 1994.

Table A14. Ecuador, Egypt

	1970	1971	1972	1973	1974	1975	1976	1977	1978	1979	1980	1981
Ecuador												
Domestic constraint	—	—	—	—	—	—	—	—	—	—	—	—
Exchange rate regime	UDP	UDP	UDP	UDP	UDP	UDP	UDP	UDP	UDP	UDP	UDP	UDP
Capital controls	Y	N	N	N	N	N	N	N	N	N	N	N
IMF program	Y[1]	Y	Y	Y	N	N	N	N	N	N	N	N
Egypt												
Domestic constraint	—	—	—	—	—	—	—	—	—	—	—	—
Exchange rate regime	BWP	BWP	BWP[2]	UDP[3]	UDP	UDP	UDP	UDP	UDP	UDP	UDP	UDP
Capital controls	Y	Y	Y	Y	Y	Y	Y	Y	Y	Y	Y	Y
IMF program	N	N	N	N	N	N	N	Y[4]	Y	Y	Y	Y

	1982	1983	1984	1985	1986	1987	1988	1989	1990	1991	1992	1993	1994
Ecuador													
Domestic constraint	—	—	—	—	—	—	—	—	—	—	—	—	—
Exchange rate regime	UDP	FL[5]	FL	FL	FL	FL	FL	FL	FL	FL	FL	FL	FL
Capital controls	N	N	N	N	Y	Y	N	N	N	N	N	N	N
IMF program	N	N	Y[6]	Y	Y	Y	Y	Y	Y	N	Y[7]	N	Y[8]
Egypt													
Domestic constraint	—	—	—	—	—	—	—	—	—	—	—	—	—
Exchange rate regime	UDP	UDP	UDP	UDP	UDP	UDP	UDP	UDP	UDP	UDP	FL[9]	FL	FL
Capital controls	Y	Y	Y	Y	Y	Y	Y	Y	Y	Y	Y	Y	Y
IMF program	N	N	N	N	N	Y[10]	Y	N	N	Y[11]	Y	Y	Y

[1]April 7, 1969–April 6, 1970; September 14, 1970–September 13, 1971; July 3, 1972–July 2, 1973.

[2]In the realignment of parities under the Smithsonian agreement, the Egyptian pound was kept constant in terms of the SDR.

[3]A multiple exchange system tied to the dollar for a major part of international transactions was introduced; the pound was devalued in early 1979 and in 1989–91. During this period, the free exchange rate depreciated more steadily. The foreign exchange reform of 1987–88 introduced a dual system (as part of this reform, on May 11, 1987, a banker's free market started operating).

[4]April 29, 1977–April 19, 1978; July 28, 1978–July 27, 1981.

[5]In March 1983, a multiple exchange rate system is introduced; the system was characterized by microdevaluations of official rates and by a free market for certain transactions.

[6]July 25, 1983–July 24, 1984; March 11, 1985–March 10, 1986; August 15, 1986–August 14, 1987; January 4, 1988–February 28, 1989; September 15, 1989–February 28, 1991.

[7]December 11, 1991–December 10, 1992.

[8]May 11, 1994–March 21, 1996.

[9]On November 28, 1991, a unified free market exchange rate was introduced; in practice, the pound has since remained stable vis-à-vis the U.S. dollar.

[10]May 15, 1987–November 30, 1988.

[11]May 17, 1991–March 1, 1993; September 20, 1993–September 19, 1996.

Table A15. Equatorial Guinea, Fiji

	1970	1971	1972	1973	1974	1975	1976	1977	1978	1979	1980	1981
Equatorial Guinea												
Domestic constraint	CU	CU	CU	CU	CU	CU	CU	CU	CU	CU	CU	CU
Exchange rate regime	FFP	FFP	FFP	FFP	FFP	FFP	FFP	FFP	FFP	FFP	FFP	FFP
Capital controls	Y	Y	Y	Y	Y	Y	Y	Y	Y	Y	Y	Y
IMF program	N	N	N	N	N	N	N	N	N	N	Y[1]	N
Fiji												
Domestic constraint	—	—	—	—	—	—	—	—	—	—	—	—
Exchange rate regime	LLP	LLP	LLP	UDP	CBP[2]	CBP	CBP	CBP	CBP	CBP	CBP	CBP
Capital controls	Y	Y	Y	Y	Y	Y	Y	Y	Y	Y	Y	Y
IMF program	N	N	N	N	N	Y[3]	N	N	N	N	N	N

	1982	1983	1984	1985	1986	1987	1988	1989	1990	1991	1992	1993	1994
Equatorial Guinea													
Domestic constraint	CU	CU	CU	CU	CU	CU	CU	CU	CU	CU	CU	CU	CU
Exchange rate regime	FFP	FFP	FFP	FFP	FFP	FFP	FFP	FFP	FFP	FFP	FFP	FFP	FFP
Capital controls	Y	Y	Y	Y	Y	Y	Y	Y	Y	Y	Y	Y	Y
IMF program	N	N	N	Y[4]	N	N	N	Y[5]	Y	Y	N	Y[6]	Y
Fiji													
Domestic constraint	—	—	—	—	—	—	—	—	—	—	—	—	—
Exchange rate regime	CBP	CBP	CBP	CBP	CBP	CBP	CBP	CBP	CBP	CBP	CBP	CBP	CBP
Capital controls	Y	Y	Y	Y	Y	Y	Y	Y	Y	Y	Y	Y	Y
IMF program	N	N	N	N	N	N	N	N	N	N	N	N	N

[1]July 1, 1980–June 30, 1981.
[2]Since April 1975, the Fiji dollar has been pegged to a basket of currencies.
[3]November 8, 1974–November 7, 1975.
[4]June 28, 1985–June 27, 1986.
[5]December 7, 1988–December 6, 1991.
[6]February 3, 1993–February 2, 1996.

Table A16. Finland, France

	1970	1971	1972	1973	1974	1975	1976	1977	1978	1979	1980	1981
Finland												
Domestic constraint	—	—	—	—	—	—	—	—	—	—	—	—
Exchange rate regime	BWP	BWP	UDP[1]	FL[2]	FL	FL	FL	FL	TWP[3]	TWP	TWP	TWP
Capital controls	Y	Y	Y	Y	Y	Y	Y	Y	Y	Y	Y	Y
IMF program	N	N	N	N	N	N	N	N	N	N	N	N
France												
Domestic constraint	—	—	—	—	—	—	—	BMT[4]	BMT	BMT	BMT	BMT
Exchange rate regime	BWP	BWP	ECM	ECM	FL[5]	FL	FL	FL	FL	ERM	ERM	ERM
Capital controls	Y	Y	Y	Y	Y	Y	Y	Y	Y	Y	Y	Y
IMF program	Y[6]	N	N	N	N	N	N	N	N	N	N	N

	1982	1983	1984	1985	1986	1987	1988	1989	1990	1991	1992	1993	1994
Finland													
Domestic constraint	—	—	—	—	—	—	—	—	—	—	—	IT[7]	IT
Exchange rate regime	TWP	TWP	TWP	TWP	TWP	TWP	TWP	TWP	TWP	EUP[8]	EUP	FL[9]	FL
Capital controls	Y	Y	Y	Y	Y	Y	Y	Y	Y	N	N	N	N
IMF program	N	N	N	N	N	N	N	N	N	N	N	N	N
France													
Domestic constraint	BMT	BMT	BMT	BMT	BMT	BMT	BMT	BMT	BMT	BMT	BMT	BMT	BMT
Exchange rate regime	ERM	ERM	ERM	ERM	ERM	ERM	ERM	ERM	ERM	ERM	ERM	ERM	ERM
Capital controls	Y	Y	Y	Y	Y	Y	Y	Y	Y	Y	Y	N	N
IMF program	N	N	N	N	N	N	N	N	N	N	N	N	N

[1]As of December 20, 1971.
[2]As of June 4, 1973.
[3]As of November 1, 1977.
[4]Before 1977, an unpublished M2 target was used by the monetary authorities; the 1977 target was announced in December 1976.
[5]As of January 1974; France rejoined the European Common Margin Arrangement between July 1975 and March 1976.
[6]September 17, 1969–September 18, 1970.
[7]First targets announced in February 1993.
[8]As of June 7, 1991.
[9]As of September 8, 1992.

Table A17. Gabon, The Gambia

	1970	1971	1972	1973	1974	1975	1976	1977	1978	1979	1980	1981
Gabon												
Domestic constraint	CU	CU	CU	CU	CU	CU	CU	CU	CU	CU	CU	CU
Exchange rate regime	FFP	FFP	FFP	FFP	FFP	FFP	FFP	FFP	FFP	FFP	FFP	FFP
Capital controls	Y	Y	Y	Y	Y	Y	Y	Y	Y	Y	Y	Y
IMF program	N	N	N	N	N	N	N	N	Y[1]	N	Y[2]	Y
The Gambia												
Domestic constraint	—	—	—	—	—	—	—	—	—	—	—	—
Exchange rate regime	BWP	BWP	LLG[3]	LLG	LLG	LLG	LLG	LLG	LLG	LLG	LLG	LLG
Capital controls	Y	Y	Y	Y	Y	Y	Y	Y	Y	Y	Y	Y
IMF program	N	N	N	N	N	N	N	Y[4]	N	Y	N	N

	1982	1983	1984	1985	1986	1987	1988	1989	1990	1991	1992	1993	1994
Gabon													
Domestic constraint	CU	CU	CU	CU	CU	CU	CU	CU	CU	CU	CU	CU	CU
Exchange rate regime	FFP	FFP	FFP	FFP	FFP	FFP	FFP	FFP	FFP	FFP	FFP	FFP	FFP
Capital controls	Y	Y	Y	Y	Y	Y	Y	Y	Y	Y	Y	Y	Y
IMF program	Y	N	N	N	N	Y[5]	Y	N	Y	Y[6]	Y	N	Y[7]
The Gambia													
Domestic constraint	—	—	—	—	—	—	—	—	—	—	BMT[8]	BMT	BMT
Exchange rate regime	LLG	LLG	LLG	LLG	LLG	LLG	FL[9]	FL	FL	FL	FL	FL	FL
Capital controls	Y	Y	Y	Y	Y	Y	Y	Y	N	N	N	N	N
IMF program	Y[10]	N	Y[11]	Y	N[12]	Y[13]	Y	Y	Y	Y	N	N	N

[1] May 31, 1978–May 30, 1979.
[2] June 27, 1980–December 31, 1982.
[3] As of May 9, 1972.
[4] May 12, 1977–May 17, 1978.
[5] December 27, 1986–December 31, 1988.
[6] September 15, 1987–March 14, 1991; September 30, 1991–March 28, 1993.
[7] March 30, 1994–March 28, 1995.
[8] In the context of an IMF-monitored program under the arrangement for enhanced consultations; however, money targets were not announced.
[9] The exchange rate was floated as of January 1986.
[10] November 2, 1978–November 1, 1980.
[11] February 22, 1982–February 21, 1983.
[12] April 23, 1984–July 22, 1985.
[13] September 17, 1986–October 16, 1987; September 17, 1987–November 10, 1990; November 12, 1988–November 21, 1991.

Table A18. Germany, Ghana

	1970	1971	1972	1973	1974	1975	1976	1977	1978	1979	1980	1981
Germany												
Domestic constraint	—	—		—	—	HMT[1]	HMT	HMT	HMT	HMT	HMT	HMT
Exchange rate regime	FL[2]	FL	BWP	FL	FL	FL	FL	FL	FL	FL	FL	FL
Capital controls	N	N	N	N	N	N	N	N	N	N	N	N
IMF program	N	N	N	N	N	N	N	N	N	N	N	N
Ghana												
Domestic constraint	—	—	—	—	—	—	—	—	—	—	—	—
Exchange rate regime	UDP[3]	UDP	UDP	UDP	UDP	UDP	UDP	UDP	UDP	UDP	UDP	UDP
Capital controls	N	N	N	N	N	N	N	N	N	N	N	N
IMF program	Y[4]	N	N	N	N	N	N	N	N	Y[5]	N	N

	1982	1983	1984	1985	1986	1987	1988	1989	1990	1991	1992	1993	1994
Germany													
Domestic constraint	HMT	HMT	HMT	HMT	HMT	HMT	BMT	BMT	BMT	BMT	BMT	BMT	BMT
Exchange rate regime	FL	FL	FL	FL	FL	FL	FL	FL	FL	FL	FL	FL	FL
Capital controls	N	N	N	N	N	N	N	N	N	N	N	N	N
IMF program	N	N	N	N	N	N	N	N	N	N	N	N	N
Ghana													
Domestic constraint	—	—	—	—	—	—	—	—	—	—	BMT	BMT	BMT
Exchange rate regime	UDP	FL[6]	FL	FL	FL	FL	FL	FL	FL	FL	FL	FL	FL
Capital controls	N	N	N	N	N	N	N	N	N	N	N	N	N
IMF program	N	N	Y[7]	Y	N	Y[8]	Y	Y	Y	Y	N[9]	N	N

[1]Targets were announced for the first time at end-1974; the targeted aggregate was currency in circulation plus required reserves, an aggregate that is close to base money.

[2]The deutsche mark floated between May 1970 and December 1971. The par was introduced on December 18, 1971, but was abandoned on March 19, 1973, when the European currency arrangement was delinked from the U.S. dollar.

[3]Before 1983, the exchange rate was pegged with infrequent step adjustments, but financial discipline was lacking and Ghana faced severe balance of payments problems and increasing black market transactions.

[4]August 1, 1969–July 20, 1970.

[5]January 10, 1979–January 9, 1980.

[6]Between April 1983 and December 1994, the exchange rate was adjusted quarterly in line with the inflation differential between Ghana and its trading partners, with a step devaluation in October 1983; between December 1994 and January 1986, the exchange rate was adjusted to achieve a real depreciation; on September 19, 1986, the exchange rate was floated in an exchange rate auction; the latter was replaced on March 19, 1992 by an interbank market.

[7]August 3, 1983–August 2, 1984; August 27, 1984–December 31, 1985.

[8]October 15, 1986–October 14, 1987; November 11, 1987–November 10, 1990; November 8, 1988–November 8, 1991; November 9, 1988–March 5, 1992.

[9]IMF-monitored program under the arrangement for enhanced consultations.

Table A19. Greece, Guatemala

	1970	1971	1972	1973	1974	1975	1976	1977	1978	1979	1980	1981
Greece												
Domestic constraint	HMT[1]	HMT	HMT	HMT	HMT	HMT	HMT	HMT	HMT	HMT	HMT	HMT
Exchange rate regime	BWP	BWP	UDP	UDP	UDP	FL[2]	FL	FL	FL	FL	FL	FL
Capital controls	Y	Y	Y	Y	Y	Y	Y	Y	Y	Y	Y	Y
IMF program	N	N	N	N	N	N	N	N	N	N	N	N
Guatemala												
Domestic constraint	—	—	—	—	—	—	—	—	—	—	—	—
Exchange rate regime	UDP	UDP	UDP	UDP	UDP	UDP	UDP	UDP	UDP	UDP	UDP	UDP
Capital controls	Y	Y	Y	N	N	N	N	N	N	N	Y	Y
IMF program	Y[3]	Y	Y	N	N	N	N	N	N	N	N	N

	1982	1983	1984	1985	1986	1987	1988	1989	1990	1991	1992	1993	1994
Greece													
Domestic constraint	BMT	BMT	BMT	BMT	BMT	BMT	BMT	BMT	BMT	BMT	BMT	BMT	BMT
Exchange rate regime	FL	FL	FL	FL	FL	FL	FL	FL	FL	FL	FL	FL	FL
Capital controls	Y	Y	Y	Y	Y	Y	Y	Y	Y	Y	Y	Y	N
IMF program	N	N	N	N	N	N	N	N	N	N	N	N	N
Guatemala													
Domestic constraint	—	—	—	—	—	—	—	—	—	—	—	BMT	BMT
Exchange rate regime	UDP	UDP	UDP	UDP	UDP	UDP	UDP	UDP	FL[4]	FL	FL	FL	FL
Capital controls	Y	Y	Y	Y	Y	Y	Y	N	N	N	N	N	N
IMF program	Y[5]	N	Y[6]	N	N	N	N	Y[7]	N	N	N	Y[8]	N

[1]A monetary program was announced in the 1950s by the Currency Committee (Zolotas (1978)); the Committee was abolished in early 1982 and its powers were transferred to the Bank of Greece; at the same time, monetary targets for broad money were announced as well as targets for domestic credit expansion.

[2]Throughout this period, the drachma was managed with respect to a basket of currencies reflecting inflation differential. As of 1988, the exchange rate policy hardened with the aim of keeping the depreciation rate in line with *targeted* inflation differential. However, only at end-1994 was the depreciation rate for the following year announced; at the same time, monetary targets were "deemphasized."

[3]August 1, 1969–July 31, 1970; December 18, 1970–December 27, 1971; March 29, 1972–March 28, 1973.

[4]As of November 31, 1989.

[5]November 13, 1981–November 12, 1982.

[6]August 31, 1983–December 31, 1984.

[7]October 26, 1988–February 29, 1990.

[8]December 18, 1992–March 17, 1994.

Table A20. Guinea, Honduras

	1970	1971	1972	1973	1974	1975	1976	1977	1978	1979	1980	1981
Guinea												
Domestic constraint	—	—	—	—	—	—	—	—	—	—	—	—
Exchange rate regime	BWP[1]	BWP	BWP	UDP	UDP	UDP	SDP	SDP	SDP	SDP	SDP	SDP
Capital controls	Y	Y	Y	Y	Y	Y	Y	Y	Y	Y	Y	Y
IMF program	N	N	N	N	N	N	N	N	N	N	N	N
Honduras												
Domestic constraint	—	—	—	—	—	—	—	—	—	—	—	—
Exchange rate regime	UDP	UDP	UDP	UDP	UDP	UDP	UDP	UDP	UDP	UDP	UDP	UDP
Capital controls	N	N	N	N	N	N	N	N	N	N	Y	Y
IMF program	N	Y[2]	Y	N	N	N	N	N	N	Y[3]	Y	Y

	1982	1983	1984	1985	1986	1987	1988	1989	1990	1991	1992	1993	1994
Guinea													
Domestic constraint	—	—	—	—	—	—	—	—	—	—	—	BMT	BMT[4]
Exchange rate regime	SDP	SDP	SDP	SDP	FL[5]	FL	FL	FL	FL	FL	FL	FL	FL
Capital controls	Y	Y	Y	Y	Y	Y	Y	Y	Y	Y	Y	Y	Y
IMF program	N	Y[6]	N	N	Y[7]	Y	Y	Y	Y	N	Y[8]	Y	Y
Honduras													
Domestic constraint	—	—	—	—	—	—	—	—	—	—	—	—	—
Exchange rate regime	UDP	UDP	UDP	UDP	UDP	UDP	UDP	UDP	UDP	UDP	FL[9]	FL	FL
Capital controls	Y	Y	Y	Y	Y	Y	Y	Y	Y	Y	Y	N	N
IMF program	Y	Y	N	N	N	N	N	N	N	Y[10]	Y	Y	Y

[1]Throughout the 1970s, parallel exchange rate markets were operating.
[2]June 1, 1971–May 3, 1972; June 2, 1972–June 6, 1973.
[3]June 28, 1979–June 27, 1982; November 5, 1982–December 31, 1983.
[4]In the Annual Report of the Central Bank of Guinea, intermediate targets for broad money began to be published.
[5]As of January 1986.
[6]December 1, 1982–December 30, 1983.
[7]February 3, 1986–March 2, 1987; July 29, 1987–July 28, 1990.
[8]November 6, 1991–November 5, 1996.
[9]The lempira was floated in May 1992.
[10]July 27, 1990–February 17, 1992; July 24, 1992–July 23, 1995.

Table A21. Iceland, India

	1970	1971	1972	1973	1974	1975	1976	1977	1978	1979	1980	1981
Iceland												
Domestic constraint	—	—	—	—	—	—	—	—	—	—	—	—
Exchange rate regime	BWP	BWP	BWP	FL[1]	FL	FL	FL	FL	FL	FL	FL	FL
Capital controls	Y	Y	Y	Y	Y	Y	Y	Y	Y	Y	Y	Y
IMF program	N	N	N	N	N	N	N	N	N	N	N	N
India												
Domestic constraint	—	—	—	—	—	—	—	—	—	—	—	—
Exchange rate regime	BWP	BWP	LLP[2]	LLP	LLP	TWP	TWP	TWP	TWP	FL[3]	FL	FL
Capital controls	Y	Y	Y	Y	Y	Y	Y	Y	Y	Y	Y	Y
IMF program	N	N	Y	N	N	N	N	N	N	N	N	N

	1982	1983	1984	1985	1986	1987	1988	1989	1990	1991	1992	1993	1994
Iceland													
Domestic constraint	—	—	—	—	—	—	—	—	—	—	—	—	—
Exchange rate regime	FL	FL[4]	FL	FL	FL	FL	FL	FL	FL	FL	CBP[5]	CBP	CBP
Capital controls	Y	Y	Y	Y	Y	Y	Y	Y	Y	Y	Y	Y	Y[6]
IMF program	N	N	N	N	N	N	N	N	N	N	N	N	N
India													
Domestic constraint	—	—	—	—	BMT[7]	BMT	BMT	BMT	BMT	BMT	BMT	BMT	BMT
Exchange rate regime	FL	FL	FL	FL	FL	FL	FL	FL	FL	FL	FL	FL	FL[8]
Capital controls	Y	Y	Y	Y	Y	Y	Y	Y	Y	Y	Y	Y	Y
IMF program	Y[9]	Y	Y	N	N	N	N	N	N	N	Y[10]	Y	Y

[1]A law issued on June 14, 1973 authorized the central bank to quote exchange rates outside the band around the par value in force until that time.

[2]Between August 22, 1971 and December 19, 1971, the rupee was pegged to the dollar. With the Smithsonian agreements of December 19, 1981, the rupee was pegged to the pound.

[3]The 2.25 percent band set around the trade-weighted peg was widened to 5 percent on January 30, 1979.

[4]Starting with the 1983 stabilization program, the exchange rate policy hardened (OECD (1990)). However, the exchange rate remained officially flexible, and the May 1985 package did not include any commitment on exchange rate policy.

[5]As of early 1992.

[6]As of January 1, 1995, all capital controls have been removed.

[7]Following the Chakravarty Report of April 1985, which recommended announcing broad money targets, the Reserve Bank of India started announcing targets in 1986; until 1990, the targets were, however, expressed only in terms of a maximum ceiling; in 1990, more specific targets were announced initially as "conditional" to the attainment of fiscal targets.

[8]As of March 1, 1993, the rupee was floated.

[9]November 11, 1981–November 8, 1984 (canceled as of May 1, 1984).

[10]October 31, 1991–June 30, 1993.

Table A22. Ireland, Indonesia

	1970	1971	1972	1973	1974	1975	1976	1977	1978	1979	1980	1981
Ireland												
Domestic constraint	—	—	—	—	—	—	—	—	—	—	—	—
Exchange rate regime	BWP	BWP	LLP[1]	LLP	LLP	LLP	LLP	LLP	LLP	ERM	ERM	ERM
Capital controls	Y	Y	Y	Y	Y	Y	Y	Y	Y	Y	Y	Y
IMF program	N	N	N	N	N	N	N	N	N	N	N	N
Indonesia												
Domestic constraint	—	—	—	—	—	—	—	—	—	—	—	—
Exchange rate regime	BWP	BWP	BWP	UDP	UDP	UDP	UDP	UDP	UDP	FL[2]	FL	FL
Capital controls	N	N	N	N	N	N	N	N	N	N	N	N
IMF program	Y[3]	Y	Y	Y	N	N	N	N	N	N	N	N

	1982	1983	1984	1985	1986	1987	1988	1989	1990	1991	1992	1993	1994
Ireland													
Domestic constraint	—	—	—	—	—	—	—	—	—	—	—	—	—
Exchange rate regime	ERM	ERM[4]	ERM	ERM	ERM	ERM	ERM	ERM	ERM	ERM	ERM	ERM	ERM
Capital controls	Y	Y	Y	Y	Y	Y	Y	Y	Y	Y	N	N	N
IMF program	N	N	N	N	N	N	N	N	N	N	N	N	N
Indonesia													
Domestic constraint	—	—	—	—	—	—	—	—	—	—	—	—	—
Exchange rate regime	FL	FL	FL	FL	FL	FL	FL	FL	FL	FL	FL	FL	FL
Capital controls	N	N	N	N	N	N	N	N	N	N	N	N	N
IMF program	N	N	N	N	N	N	N	N	N	N	N	N	N

[1]As of May 9, 1992.

[2]The peg of the Indonesian rupiah was severed on November 15, 1978; since then, the rupiah has followed a managed float in which it was depreciated in line with the inflation differential. A band is maintained around the crawling peg.

[3]April 14, 1969–April 16, 1971; April 22, 1971–April 21, 1972; April 17, 1972–April 16, 1973; May 4, 1973–May 3, 1974.

[4]The early 1982 stabilization did not involve any change in the monetary policy framework.

Table A23. Israel, Italy

	1970	1971	1972	1973	1974	1975	1976	1977	1978	1979	1980	1981
Israel												
Domestic constraint	—	—	—	—	—	—	—	—	—	—	—	—
Exchange rate regime	BWP	BWP	UDP	UDP	FL	FL	FL	FL	FL	FL	FL	FL
Capital controls	Y	Y	Y	Y	Y	Y	Y	Y	Y	Y	Y	Y
IMF program	N	N	N	N	N	Y[1]	N	Y[2]	N	N	N	N
Italy												
Domestic constraint	—	—	—	—	DCT[3]	DCT	DCT	DCT	DCT	DCT	DCT	DCT
Exchange rate regime	BWP	BWP	ECM[4]	FL	FL	FL	FL	FL	FL	ERM	ERM	ERM
Capital controls	Y	Y	Y	Y	Y	Y	Y	Y	Y	Y	Y	Y
IMF program	N	N	N	N	Y[5]	N	N	Y[6]	Y	N	N	N

	1982	1983	1984	1985	1986	1987	1988	1989	1990	1991	1992	1993	1994
Israel													
Domestic constraint	—	—	—	—	—	—	—	—	—	—[7]	—	—	—
Exchange rate regime	FL	FL	FL	FL	UDP[8]	CBP[9]	CBP	CBP	CBP	CBP	CBCP	CBCP	CBCP
Capital controls	Y	Y	Y	Y	Y	Y	Y	Y	Y	Y	Y	Y	Y
IMF program	N	N	N	N	N	N	N	N	N	N	N	N	N
Italy													
Domestic constraint	DCT	DCT	DCT	BMT[10]	BMT	BMT	BMT	BMT	BMT	BMT	BMT	BMT	BMT
Exchange rate regime	ERM	ERM	ERM	ERM	ERM	ERM	ERM	ERM	ERM	ERM	ERM	FL[11]	FL
Capital controls	Y	Y	Y	Y	Y	Y	Y	Y	Y	Y	Y	N	N
IMF program	N	N	N	N	N	N	N	N	N	N	N	N	N

[1]November 8, 1974–November 7, 1975; February 14, 1975–February 13, 1976.

[2]October 20, 1976–October 19, 1977.

[3]A target on total domestic credit was set initially as part of an IMF-supported program.

[4]Italy abandoned the arrangement in February 1973.

[5]April 10, 1974–April 9, 1975.

[6]April 25, 1977–December 31, 1978.

[7]As of December 1991, annual inflation targets have been announced, initially in connection with the announced depreciation rate; but no formal procedure for medium-term inflation targeting was introduced.

[8]The peg was introduced with the July 1985 stabilization package (Bufman and others (1994)); after some step devaluations, an exchange rate band was introduced on January 3, 1989; the band was widened in March 1990; in December 1991, a crawling peg was introduced (at the same time, Israel shifted from "other composite" to "managed float" in the *International Financial Statistics* definitions).

[9]As of August 1986.

[10]Targets for M2 and private domestic credit have been announced as of 1985; subsequently, the private domestic credit target was dropped; as of 1986, the target for DCT was dropped.

[11]As of September 16, 1992.

Table A24. Côte d'Ivoire (Ivory Coast), Jamaica

	1970	1971	1972	1973	1974	1975	1976	1977	1978	1979	1980	1981
Côte d'Ivoire												
Domestic constraint	CU	CU	CU	CU	CU	CU	CU	CU	CU	CU	CU	CU
Exchange rate regime	FFP	FFP	FFP	FFP	FFP	FFP	FFP	FFP	FFP	FFP	FFP	FFP
Capital controls	Y	Y	Y	Y	Y	Y	Y	Y	Y	Y	Y	Y
IMF program	N	N	N	N	N	N	N	N	N	N	N	Y[1]
Jamaica												
Domestic constraint	—	—	—	—	—	—	—	—	—	—	—	—
Exchange rate regime	BWP	BWP	LLP	UDP[2]	UDP	UDP	UDP	UDP	UDCP[3]	UDP[4]	UDP	UDP
Capital controls	Y	Y	Y	Y	Y	Y	Y	Y	Y	Y	Y	Y
IMF program	N	N	N	Y[5]	N	N	N	N	Y[6]	Y	Y	Y

	1982	1983	1984	1985	1986	1987	1988	1989	1990	1991	1992	1993	1994
Côte d'Ivoire													
Domestic constraint	CU	CU	CU	CU	CU	CU	CU	CU	CU	CU	CU	CU	CU
Exchange rate regime	FFP	FFP	FFP	FFP	FFP	FFP	FFP	FFP	FFP	FFP	FFP	FFP	FFP
Capital controls	Y	Y	Y	Y	Y	Y	Y	Y	Y	Y	Y	Y	Y
IMF program	Y	Y	Y	Y	N	N	N	N	N	N	N	N	Y[7]
Jamaica													
Domestic constraint	—	—	—	—	—	—	—	—	—	—	—	—	—
Exchange rate regime	UDP	UDP	UDP[8]	UDP[9]	UDP	UDP	UDP	UDP	FL[10]	FL	FL	FL	FL
Capital controls	Y	Y	Y	Y	Y	Y	Y	Y	Y	Y	Y	Y	Y
IMF program	Y	Y	Y	Y	Y	Y	Y	Y	Y	Y	Y	Y	Y

[1]February 27, 1981–February 22, 1984; August 3, 1984–May 2, 1985; June 3, 1985–June 2, 1986.

[2]Unfrequent but relatively large adjustments were undertaken periodically within a dual exchange rate system.

[3]Between June 9, 1978–May 2, 1979.

[4]Within a multiple exchange rate system.

[5]June 1, 1973–May 3, 1974.

[6]August 11, 1977–August 10, 1979; June 9, 1978–June 8, 1981; April 13, 1981–April 12, 1984; June 22, 1984–June 21, 1985; July 17, 1985–May 31, 1987; March 2, 1987–May 31, 1988; September 19, 1988–May 31, 1990; March 23, 1990–May 31, 1991; June 28, 1991–June 30, 1992; December 11, 1992–December 10, 1995.

[7]March 11, 1994–March 10, 1997.

[8]On November 24, 1984, the exchange rate system was unified; a band was established around the parity, which was revised fortnightly.

[9]As of November 29, 1984, the Jamaican dollar was officially floating in an auction, but the exchange rate was practically fixed by intervention at 5.5 Jamaican dollars per U.S. dollar; this regime lasted until mid-1989 when the exchange rate started depreciating.

[10]As of September 17, 1990, the exchange rate was determined in an interbank market.

Table A25. Japan, Jordan

	1970	1971	1972	1973	1974	1975	1976	1977	1978	1979	1980	1981
Japan												
Domestic constraint	—	—	—	—	—	—	—	—	—[1]	—	—	—
Exchange rate regime	BWP	BWP	BWP	FL	FL	FL	FL	FL	FL	FL	FL	FL
Capital controls	Y	Y	Y	Y	Y	Y	Y	Y	Y	N	N	N
IMF program	N	N	N	N	N	N	N	N	N	N	N	N
Jordan												
Domestic constraint	—	—	—	—	—	—	—	—	—	—	—	—
Exchange rate regime	BWP	BWP	BWP	SDP[2]	SDP	SDP	SDP	SDP	SDP	SDP	SDP	SDP
Capital controls	Y	Y	Y	Y	Y	Y	Y	Y	Y	Y	Y	Y
IMF program	N	N	N	N	N	N	N	N	N	N	N	N

	1982	1983	1984	1985	1986	1987	1988	1989	1990	1991	1992	1993	1994
Japan													
Domestic constraint	—	—	—	—	—	—	—	—[3]	—	—	—	—	—
Exchange rate regime	FL	FL	FL	FL	FL	FL	FL	FL	FL	FL	FL	FL	FL
Capital controls	N	N	N	N	N	N	N	N	N	N	N	N	N
IMF program	N	N	N	N	N	N	N	N	N	N	N	N	N
Jordan													
Domestic constraint	—	—	—	—	—	—	—	—	—	—	—	—	—
Exchange rate regime	SDP	SDP	SDP	SDP	SDP	SDP	SDP[4]	CBP[5]	CBP	CBP	CBP	CBP	CBP
Capital controls	Y	Y	Y	Y	Y	Y	Y	Y	Y	Y	Y	Y	Y
IMF program	N	N	N	N	N	N	N	N	Y[6]	Y	Y	Y	Y

[1]Quarterly projections for broad money began to be published.

[2]Officially the peg started only on February 15, 1975, with margins of 2.25 percent.

[3]The emphasis on money declined as of the late 1990s (Sawamoto and Ichikawa (1994)).

[4]The dinar floated during October 1988–February 7, 1989.

[5]The peg was officially introduced in May 1989; a dual pegged exchange rate system was in place during July 31, 1989–February 17, 1990.

[6]July 14, 1989–January 31, 1991; February 26, 1992–February 25, 1994; May 25, 1994–May 24, 1997.

Table A26. Kenya, Kiribati

	1970	1971	1972	1973	1974	1975	1976	1977	1978	1979	1980	1981
Kenya												
Domestic constraint	—	—	—	—	—	—	—	—	—	—	—	—
Exchange rate regime	BWP	BWP	UDP[1]	UDP	UDP	UDP	SDP[2]	SDP	SDP	SDP	SDP	SDP
Capital controls	Y	Y	Y	Y	Y	Y	Y	Y	Y	Y	Y	Y
IMF program	N	N	N	N	N	N	Y[3]	Y	Y	Y	Y	Y
Kiribati												
Domestic constraint	FC[4]	FC	FC	FC	FC	FC	FC	FC	FC	FC	FC	FC
Exchange rate regime	AUP[4]	AUP	AUP	AUP	AUP	AUP	AUP	AUP	AUP	AUP	AUP	AUP
Capital controls	N	N	N	N	N	N	N	N	N	N	N	N
IMF program	N	N	N	N	N	N	N	N	N	N	N	N

	1982	1983	1984	1985	1986	1987	1988	1989	1990	1991	1992	1993	1994
Kenya													
Domestic constraint	—	—	—	—	—	—	—	—	—	—	—	—	—
Exchange rate regime	SDP	FL[5]	FL	FL	FL	FL	FL	FL	FL	FL	FL	FL	FL
Capital controls	Y	Y	Y	Y	Y	Y	Y	Y	Y	Y	Y	Y	Y
IMF program	Y	Y	Y	Y	N	N	Y[6]	Y	Y	Y	Y	Y	Y
Kiribati													
Domestic constraint	FC	FC	FC	FC	FC	FC	FC	FC	FC	FC	FC	FC	FC
Exchange rate regime	AUP	AUP	AUP	AUP	AUP	AUP	AUP	AUP	AUP	AUP	AUP	AUP	AUP
Capital controls	N	N	N	N	N	N	N	N	N	N	N	N	N
IMF program	N	N	N	N	N	N	N	N	N	N	N	N	N

[1]The exchange rate was briefly pegged to the U.K. sterling after the Smithsonian agreement.

[2]As of October 1975.

[3]July 7, 1975–June 7, 1978; November 13, 1978–November 12, 1979; August 20, 1979–August 19, 1981; October 15, 1980–October 14, 1982; January 8, 1982–January 7, 1983; March 21, 1983–September 20, 1984; February 5, 1985–February 7, 1986.

[4]Except for a small amount of coins, there is no issue of currency in Kiribati. The Australian dollar is used as legal tender.

[5]As of December 1982, the exchange rate was floated.

[6]February 1, 1988–July 31, 1989; May 15, 1989–March 31, 1993; October 1, 1993–September 30, 1994.

Table A27. Korea, Lebanon

	1970	1971	1972	1973	1974	1975	1976	1977	1978	1979	1980	1981
Korea												
Domestic constraint	—	—	—	—	—	—	—	—	—	BMT	BMT	BMT
Exchange rate regime	FL	FL	FL	FL	UDP	UDP	UDP	UDP	UDP	UDP	FL	FL
Capital controls	Y	Y	Y	Y	Y	Y	Y	Y	Y	Y	Y	Y
IMF program	Y[1]	Y	Y	Y[2]	Y[3]	N	Y[4]	Y[5]	N	N	Y[6]	Y
Lebanon												
Domestic constraint	—	—	—	—	—	—	—	—	—	—	—	—
Exchange rate regime	FL[7]	FL	FL	FL	FL	FL	FL	FL	FL	FL	FL	FL
Capital controls	N	N	N	N	N	N	N	N	N	N	N	N
IMF program	N	N	N	N	N	N	N	N	N	N	N	N

	1982	1983	1984	1985	1986	1987	1988	1989	1990	1991	1992	1993	1994
Korea													
Domestic constraint	BMT	BMT	BMT	BMT	BMT	BMT	BMT	BMT	BMT	BMT	BMT	BMT	BMT
Exchange rate regime	FL	FL	FL	FL	FL	FL	FL	FL	FL	FL	FL	FL	FL
Capital controls	Y	Y	Y	Y	Y	Y	Y	Y	Y	Y	Y	Y	Y
IMF program	N	Y[8]	Y	Y	Y	N	N	N	N	N	N	N	N
Lebanon													
Domestic constraint	—	—	—	—	—	—	—	—	—	—	—	—	—
Exchange rate regime	FL	FL	FL	FL	FL	FL	FL	FL	FL	FL	FL	FL	FL
Capital controls	N	N	N	N	N	N	N	N	N	N	N	N	N
IMF program	N	N	N	N	N	N	N	N	N	N	N	N	N

[1] March 13, 1970–December 31, 1970; January 1, 1971–December 31, 1971; January 1, 1972–December 31, 1972.
[2] April 2, 1973–December 31, 1973.
[3] May 17, 1974–December 31, 1974.
[4] October 22, 1975–June 30, 1976.
[5] May 6, 1977–December 31, 1977.
[6] March 3, 1980–March 2, 1982.
[7] A floating exchange rate regime was introduced in 1952.
[8] July 8, 1983–March 1, 1985; July 12, 1985–March 10, 1987.

Table A28. Lesotho, Malawi

	1970	1971	1972	1973	1974	1975	1976	1977	1978	1979	1980	1981
Lesotho												
Domestic constraint	FC[1]	FC	FC	FC	FC	FC	FC	FC	FC	CB[2]	CB	CB
Exchange rate regime	SRP[1]	SRP	SRP	SRP	SRP	SRP	SRP	SRP	SRP	SRP	SRP[2]	SRP
Capital controls	N	N	N	N	N	N	N	N	N	N	N	N
IMF program	N	N	N	N	N	N	N	N	N	N	N	N
Malawi												
Domestic constraint	—	—	—	—	—	—	—	—	—	—	—	—
Exchange rate regime	BWP	BWP	LLP[3]	LLP	LLP	SDP	SDP	SDP	SDP	SDP	SDP	SDP
Capital controls	Y	Y	Y	Y	Y	Y	Y	Y	Y	Y	Y	Y
IMF program	N	N	N	N	N	N	N	N	N	N	Y[4]	Y

	1982	1983	1984	1985	1986	1987	1988	1989	1990	1991	1992	1993	1994
Lesotho													
Domestic constraint	CB	CB	CB	CB	CB	CB	CB	CB	CB	CB	CB	CB	CB
Exchange rate regime	SRP	SRP	SRP	SRP	SRP[5]	SRP	SRP	SRP	SRP	SRP	SRP	SRP	SRP
Capital controls	N	N	N	N	N	N	N	N	N	N	N	N	N
IMF program	N	N	N	N	N	N	N	Y[6]	Y	Y	Y	Y	Y
Malawi													
Domestic constraint	—	—	—	—	—	—	—	—	—	—	—	—	—
Exchange rate regime	SDP	SDP	FL[7]	FL	FL	FL	FL	FL	FL	FL	FL	FL	FL[8]
Capital controls	Y	Y	Y	Y	Y	Y	Y	Y	Y	Y	Y	Y	Y
IMF program	Y	Y	Y	Y	Y	N	Y[9]	Y	Y	Y	Y	Y	Y

[1]The South African rand was the sole legal tender.

[2]On January 19, 1990, the Lesotho Monetary Authority (as of 1982, the Central Bank of Lesotho) was opened, and a domestic currency (the loti) was introduced. The rand remained legal tender. The central bank started issuing currency backed by gold or foreign reserves (until March 31, 1986, only reserves in rand could be held; later, 35 percent of reserves could be held in convertible currency).

[3]As of May 9, 1972.

[4]October 31, 1979–December 31, 1981; May 9, 1980–March 31, 1982; August 6, 1982–August 5, 1983; September 19, 1983–September 18, 1986.

[5]As of 1986, the parity with the rand can be altered.

[6]July 5, 1988–June 28, 1991; May 22, 1991–August 1, 1994; September 23, 1994–September 22, 1995.

[7]In January 1984, the kwacha was pegged to an undisclosed basket of currencies; the parities were, however, revised frequently.

[8]In February 1994, the exchange rate was floated.

[9]March 2, 1988–May 30, 1989; July 15, 1988–March 31, 1994; November 16, 1994–June 30, 1995.

Table A29. Malaysia, Maldives

	1970	1971	1972	1973	1974	1975	1976	1977	1978	1979	1980	1981
Malaysia												
Domestic constraint	—[1]	—	—	—	—	—	—	—	—	—	—	—
Exchange rate regime	LLP	LLP	UDP[2]	FL[3]	FL	FL[4]	FL	FL[5]	FL	FL	FL	FL
Capital controls	Y	Y	Y	N	N	N	N	N	N	N	N	N
IMF program	N	N	N	N	N	N	N	N	N	N	N	N
Maldives												
Domestic constraint	—	—	—	—	—	—	—	—	—	—	—[6]	—
Exchange rate regime	FL[7]	FL	FL	FL	FL	FL	FL	FL	FL	UDP[8]	UDP	UDP
Capital controls	N	N	N	N	N	N	N	N	N	N	N	N
IMF program	N	N	N	N	N	N	N	N	N	N	N	N

	1982	1983	1984	1985	1986	1987	1988	1989	1990	1991	1992	1993	1994
Malaysia													
Domestic constraint	—	—	—	—	—	—	—	—	—	—	—	—	—
Exchange rate regime	FL	FL	FL	FL	FL	FL	FL	FL	FL	FL	FL[9]	FL	
Capital controls	N	N	N	N	N	N	N	N	N	N	N	N	N
IMF program	N	N	N	N	N	N	N	N	N	N	N	N	N
Maldives													
Domestic constraint	—	—	—	—	—	—	—	—	—	—	—	—	—
Exchange rate regime	UDP	UDP	UDP	UDP	TWP[10]	FL[11]	FL	FL	FL	FL	FL	FL	
Capital controls	N	N	N	N	N	N	N	N	N	N	N	N	N
IMF program	N	N	N	N	N	N	N	N	N	N	N	N	N

[1]A currency board was in place until 1967.

[2]As of June 24, 1972.

[3]The Malaysian dollar (ringgit as of August 28, 1975) was allowed to float on June 21, 1973.

[4]As of September 27, 1975, a managed float around an undisclosed basket of currencies was followed; in some cases, this policy is described as a "peg," but it is clear that the authorities never relied on a fixed formula to decide their intervention (Aghevli (1982)); however, in the early and mid-1980s, the exchange rate became more relevant (see Yan (1971)).

[5]In 1977, Malaysia advised the IMF that the exchange rate regime would shift to a trade-weighted peg.

[6]On July 1, 1991, the Maldives Monetary Authority was established and took over the functions of currency issues of the Department of Finance.

[7]Before 1979, the exchange rate was floating.

[8]In April 1979, a dual fixed exchange rate system was introduced. Starting in 1982, the exchange rate system was progressively unified.

[9]In 1993, the Malaysian authorities advised the IMF that the exchange rate regime was managed floating.

[10]As of July 1985.

[11]On March 1, 1987, the rufiyaa was devalued and since then, the exchange rate has been allowed to move broadly in line with market forces, albeit with varying degrees of periodic official intervention. For internal purposes, the Maldives Monetary Authority has sometimes used exchange rate target bands.

Table A30. Mali, Malta

	1970	1971	1972	1973	1974	1975	1976	1977	1978	1979	1980	1981
Mali												
Domestic constraint	—	—	—	—	—	—	—	—	—	—	—	—
Exchange rate regime	FFP	FFP	FFP	FFP	FFP	FFP	FFP	FFP	FFP	FFP	FFP	FFP
Capital controls	Y	Y	Y	Y	Y	Y	Y	Y	Y	Y	Y	Y
IMF program	Y[1]	Y	Y	N	N	N	N	N	N	N	N	N
Malta												
Domestic constraint	—	—	—	—	—	—	—	—	—	—	—	—
Exchange rate regime	BWP	BWP	FL[2]	TWP	TWP	TWP	TWP	TWP	TWP	TWP	TWP	TWP
Capital controls	Y	Y	Y	Y	Y	Y	Y	Y	Y	Y	Y	Y
IMF program	N	N	N	N	N	N	N	N	N	N	N	N

	1982	1983	1984	1985	1986	1987	1988	1989	1990	1991	1992	1993	1994
Mali													
Domestic constraint	—	—	CU[3]	CU	CU	CU	CU	CU	CU	CU	CU	CU	CU
Exchange rate regime	FFP	FFP	FFP	FFP	FFP	FFP	FFP	FFP	FFP	FFP	FFP	FFP	FFP
Capital controls	Y	Y	Y	Y	Y	Y	Y	Y	Y	Y	Y	Y	Y
IMF program	Y[4]	Y	Y	Y	Y	N	N	Y[5]	Y	Y	N	Y[6]	Y
Malta													
Domestic constraint	—	—	—	—	—	—	—	—	—	—	—	—	—
Exchange rate regime	TWP	TWP	TWP	TWP	TWP	TWP	TWP	TWP	TWP	TWP	TWP	TWP	TWP
Capital controls	Y	Y	Y	Y	Y	Y	Y	Y	Y	Y	Y	Y	Y
IMF program	N	N	N	N	N	N	N	N	N	N	N	N	N

[1]October 23, 1969–October 22, 1970; July 20, 1971–July 28, 1972.

[2]The lira was floated between May 9, 1972 and March 1973, when a trade-weighted peg was announced. Malta is considered to have been the first country to introduce such an exchange rate peg (Joseph (1992)).

[3]As of June 1, 1984, Mali rejoined the West African Monetary Union.

[4]May 21, 1982–May 20, 1983; December 9, 1983–May 31, 1985; November 8, 1985–March 31, 1987.

[5]August 5, 1988–August 4, 1991.

[6]August 28, 1991–August 27, 1995.

Table A31. Mauritius, Mexico

	1970	1971	1972	1973	1974	1975	1976	1977	1978	1979	1980	1981
Mauritius												
Domestic constraint	—	—	—	—	—	—	—	—	—	—	—	—
Exchange rate regime	BWP	BWP	LLP[1]	LLP	LLP	LLP	LLP	SDP	SDP	SDP	SDP	SDP
Capital controls	Y	Y	Y	Y	Y	Y	Y	Y	Y	Y	Y	Y
IMF program	N	N	N	N	N	N	N	N	Y[2]	Y	Y	Y
Mexico												
Domestic constraint	—	—	—	—	—	—	—	—	—	—	—	—
Exchange rate regime	UDP	UDP	UDP	UDP	UDP	UDP	UDP	FL	FL	FL	FL	FL
Capital controls	N	N	N	N	N	N	N	N	N	N	N	N
IMF program	N	N	N	N	N	N	N	Y[3]	Y	Y	N	N

	1982	1983	1984	1985	1986	1987	1988	1989	1990	1991	1992	1993	1994
Mauritius													
Domestic constraint	—	—	—	—	—	—	—	—	—	—	—	—	—
Exchange rate regime	SDP	FL[4]	FL	FL	FL	FL	FL	FL	FL	FL	FL	FL	FL
Capital controls	Y	Y	Y	Y	Y	Y	Y	Y	Y	Y	Y	Y	Y
IMF program	Y	Y	Y	Y	Y	N	N	N	N	N	N	N	N
Mexico													
Domestic constraint	—	—	—	—	—	—	—	—	—	—	—	—	—
Exchange rate regime	UDP	FL	FL	FL	FL	FL	UDCP[5]	UDCP	UDP	UDP	UDP	UDP	UDP
Capital controls	N	Y	Y	Y	Y	Y	Y	Y	Y	Y	Y	Y	Y
IMF program	N	Y[6]	Y	Y	N	Y[7]	N	Y[8]	Y	Y	N	N	N

[1]As of May 9, 1972, the rupee was floated together with the sterling.

[2]February 24, 1987–February 23, 1979; October 31, 1979–October 30, 1981; September 5, 1980–September 4, 1981; December 21, 1981–December 20, 1982; May 18, 1983–August 17, 1984; March 1, 1985–August 31, 1986.

[3]January 1, 1977–December 31, 1979.

[4]On February 24, 1983, the rupee was pegged to an undisclosed currency basket, with realignments to adjust for inflation differentials.

[5]The economic solidarity pact of December 1987 introduced an exchange rate peg; in January 1989, the peg was replaced by a crawling peg; on November 11, 1991, an exchange rate band was introduced (Helpman and others (1994)).

[6]January 1, 1983–December 31, 1985.

[7]November 1986–April 1988.

[8]May 26, 1989–May 25, 1992.

Table A32. Morocco, Nepal

	1970	1971	1972	1973	1974	1975	1976	1977	1978	1979	1980	1981
Morocco												
Domestic constraint	—	—	—	—	—	—	—	—	—	—	BMT	BMT
Exchange rate regime	BWP	BWP	BWP	TWP[1]	TWP	TWP	TWP	TWP	TWP	TWP	FL[2]	FL
Capital controls	Y	Y	Y	Y	Y	Y	Y	Y	Y	Y	Y	Y
IMF program	Y[3]	Y	N	N	N	N	N	N	N	N	N	Y[4]
Nepal												
Domestic constraint	—	—	—	—	—	—	—	—	—	—	—	—
Exchange rate regime	BWP	BWP	UDP[5]	UDP	SDP[6]	UDP[7]	UDP	UDP	UDP	UDP	UDP	UDP
Capital controls	Y	Y	Y	Y	Y	Y	Y	Y	Y	Y	Y	Y
IMF program	N	N	N	N	N	N	Y[8]	N	N	N	N	N

	1982	1983	1984	1985	1986	1987	1988	1989	1990	1991	1992	1993	1994
Morocco													
Domestic constraint	BMT	BMT	BMT	BMT	BMT	BMT	BMT	BMT	BMT	BMT	—	—	—
Exchange rate regime	FL	FL	FL	FL	FL	FL	FL	FL	TWP[9]	TWP	TWP	TWP	TWP
Capital controls	Y	Y	Y	Y	Y	Y	Y	Y	Y	Y	Y	Y	Y
IMF program	Y	Y	Y	Y	Y	Y	Y	Y	Y	N	Y[10]	N	N
Nepal													
Domestic constraint	—	—	—	—	—	—	—	—	—	—	—	—	—
Exchange rate regime	UDP	CBP[11]	CBP	CBP	CBP	CBP	CBP	CBP	CBP	CBP	IRP[12]	IRP	IRP
Capital controls	Y	Y	Y	Y	Y	Y	Y	Y	Y	Y	Y	Y	Y
IMF program	N	N	N	N	Y[13]	Y	Y	Y	Y	Y	N	Y[14]	Y

[1]In May 1973, Morocco adopted a trade-weighted peg.

[2]Starting in 1980, the dinar was rapidly depreciated against the trade-weighted basket; up to 1986, the depreciation more than offset inflation differentials; between 1987 and early 1990, the depreciation was in line with inflation differentials.

[3]December 15, 1969–December 14, 1970; March 18, 1971–March 17, 1972.

[4]October 8, 1980–October 7, 1983; September 16, 1983–March 15, 1985; September 12, 1985–February 28, 1987; December 16, 1986–March 31, 1988; August 30, 1988–December 31, 1989; July 20, 1990–March 31, 1991.

[5]Following the Smithsonian realignment, in December 1991, the rupee was pegged to the U.S. dollar.

[6]As of July 16, 1973.

[7]As of June 30, 1975.

[8]February 18, 1976–February 17, 1977.

[9]After the May 1990 devaluation, the dirham remained pegged to the trade-weighted basket.

[10]January 31, 1992–March 31, 1993.

[11]The currency basket was introduced on June 1, 1983.

[12]The peg was introduced on July 2, 1991; a dual exchange rate with a market-determined rate for most current account transactions was in place between March 2, 1992 and February 1993.

[13]December 23, 1985–April 22, 1987; October 14, 1987–October 13, 1990.

[14]October 5, 1992–October 4, 1995.

Table A33. Netherlands, New Zealand

	1970	1971	1972	1973	1974	1975	1976	1977	1978	1979	1980	1981
Netherlands												
Domestic constraint	—	—	—	—	—	—	—	—	—	—	—	—
Exchange rate regime	FL[1]	FL	ECM	ECM	ECM	ECM	ECM	ECM	ECM	ERM	ERM	ERM
Capital controls	Y	Y	Y	Y	Y	Y	Y	N	N	N	N	N
IMF program	N	N	N	N	N	N	N	N	N	N	N	N
New Zealand												
Domestic constraint	—	—	—	—	—	—	—	—	—[2]	—	—	—
Exchange rate regime	BW	BW	BW	UDP	TWP[3]	TWP	TWP	TWP	TWP	FL[4]	FL	FL
Capital controls	Y	Y	Y	Y	Y	Y	Y	Y	Y	Y	Y	Y
IMF program	N	N	N	N	N	N	N	N	N	N	N	N

	1982	1983	1984	1985	1986	1987	1988	1989	1990	1991	1992	1993	1994
Netherlands													
Domestic constraint	—	—	—	—	—	—	—	—	—	—	—	—	—
Exchange rate regime	ERM	ERM	ERM	ERM	ERM	ERM	ERM	ERM	ERM	ERM	ERM	ERM	ERM
Capital controls	N	N	N	N	N	N	N	N	N	N	N	N	N
IMF program	N	N	N	N	N	N	N	N	N	N	N	N	N
New Zealand													
Domestic constraint	—	—	—	—	—	—	—	—	IT	IT	IT	IT	IT
Exchange rate regime	TWP	TWP	TWP	FL[5]	FL	FL	FL	FL	FL	FL	FL	FL	FL
Capital controls	Y	Y	N	N	N	N	N	N	N	N	N	N	N
IMF program	N	N	N	N	N	N	N	N	N	N	N	N	N

[1]The exchange rate was floated in May 1970; the parity was reintroduced on December 19, 1971.

[2]In the second half of the 1970s, the Central Bank of New Zealand started preparing projections for domestic credit expansion and broad money. These projections were deemed too unreliable to be published (Reserve Bank of New Zealand (1979)), page 11). Only in August 1978 did the Ministry of Finance publish guidelines for private bank credit with the aim of influencing expectations.

[3]As of July 1973.

[4]A crawling peg with respect to a trade-weighted basket was introduced between June 1979 and June 1982; the rate of crawl was not announced but was adjusted to inflation differentials.

[5]A floating exchange rate was introduced in March 1985, following the removal of exchange rate controls.

Table A34. Niger, Nigeria

	1970	1971	1972	1973	1974	1975	1976	1977	1978	1979	1980	1981
Niger												
Domestic constraint	CU	CU	CU	CU	CU	CU	CU	CU	CU	CU	CU	CU
Exchange rate regime	FFP	FFP	FFP	FFP	FFP	FFP	FFP	FFP	FFP	FFP	FFP	FFP
Capital controls	Y	Y	Y	Y	Y	Y	Y	Y	Y	Y	Y	Y
IMF program	N	N	N	N	N	N	N	N	N	N	N	N
Nigeria												
Domestic constraint	—	—	—	—	—	—	—	—	—	—	—	—
Exchange rate regime	BWT	BWT	BWT	BWT	FL[1]	FL	FL	FL	FL	FL	FL	FL
Capital controls	Y	Y	Y	Y	Y	Y	Y	Y	Y	Y	Y	Y
IMF program	N	N	N	N	N	N	N	N	N	N	N	N

	1982	1983	1984	1985	1986	1987	1988	1989	1990	1991	1992	1993	1994
Niger													
Domestic constraint	CU	CU	CU	CU	CU	CU	CU	CU	CU	CU	CU	CU	CU
Exchange rate regime	FFP	FFP	FFP	FFP	FFP	FFP	FFP	FFP	FFP	FFP	FFP	FFP	FFP
Capital controls	Y	Y	Y	Y	Y	Y	Y	Y	Y	Y	Y	Y	Y
IMF program	N	N	Y[2]	Y	Y	Y	Y	Y	Y	Y	N	N	Y[3]
Nigeria													
Domestic constraint	—	—	—	—	—	NMT	NMT	NMT	NMT	NMT	NMT	NMT	NMT
Exchange rate regime	FL	FL	FL	FL	FL	FL	FL	FL	FL	FL	FL	FL	UDP[4]
Capital controls	Y	Y	Y	Y	Y	Y	Y	Y	Y	Y	Y	Y	Y
IMF program	N	N	N	N	N	Y[5]	N	Y[6]	N	Y[7]	N	N	N

[1]As of April 1974, the naira rate was administratively determined by the authorities with reference to the changes in value of a preselected group of currencies. At the same date, the IMF was notified that the fluctuations of the naira would not be held anymore within predetermined margins. In the second half of 1986, a more flexible regime based on exchange rate auctions was introduced.

[2]October 5, 1983–December 4, 1984; December 5, 1984–December 4, 1985; December 5, 1985–December 4, 1986; December 5, 1986–December 4, 1987; November 17, 1986–November 16, 1989; December 12, 1988–December 11, 1991.

[3]March 4, 1994–March 3, 1995.

[4]Introduced in early 1994.

[5]January 30, 1987–January 31, 1988.

[6]February 3, 1989–April 30, 1990.

[7]January 9, 1991–April 8, 1992.

Table A35. Norway, Oman

	1970	1971	1972	1973	1974	1975	1976	1977	1978	1979	1980	1981
Norway												
Domestic constraint	—	—	—	—	—	—	—	—	—	—	—	—
Exchange rate regime	BWP	BWP	ECM	ECM	ECM	ECM	ECM	ECM	ECM	TWB[1]	TWB	TWB
Capital controls	Y	Y	Y	Y	Y	Y	Y	Y	Y	Y	Y	Y
IMF program	N	N	N	N	N	N	N	N	N	N	N	N
Oman												
Domestic constraint	CB	CB	CB	CB	—[2]	—	—	—	—	—	—	—
Exchange rate regime	GLP[3]	GLP	GLP	UDP[4]	UDP	UDP	UDP	UDP	UDP	UDP	UDP	UDP
Capital controls	N	N	N	N	N	N	N	N	N	N	N	N
IMF program	N	N	N	N	N	N	N	N	N	N	N	N

	1982	1983	1984	1985	1986	1987	1988	1989	1990	1991	1992	1993	1994
Norway													
Domestic constraint	—	—	—	—	—	—	—	—	—	—	—	—	—
Exchange rate regime	TWB	TWB	TWB	TWB	TWB	TWB	TWB	TWB	TWB	EUP[5]	EUP	FL[6]	FL[7]
Capital controls	Y	Y	Y	Y	Y	Y	Y	Y	N	N	N	N	N
IMF program	N	N	N	N	N	N	N	N	N	N	N	N	N
Oman													
Domestic constraint	—	—	—	—	—	—	—	—	—	—	—	—	—
Exchange rate regime	UDP	UDP	UDP	UDP	UDP	UDP	UDP	UDP	UDP	UDP	UDP	UDP	UDP
Capital controls	N	N	N	N	N	N	N	N	N	N	N	N	N
IMF program	N	N	Y[4]	N	N	N	N	N	N	N	N	N	N

[1]As of December 12, 1978.

[2]In 1974, the Central Bank of Oman replaced the existing currency board.

[3]The rial saidi (rial Omani as of 1972) was introduced on May 7, 1970; the par value was expressed in terms of grams of fine gold.

[4]As of February 1973.

[5]As of October 22, 1990.

[6]As of December 10, 1992.

[7]In May 1994, the government issued new monetary policy guidelines according to which monetary and exchange policies would be aimed at maintaining the krone exchange rate broadly stable against the ECU; however, there would not be any commitment to defend a specific parity (see Norges Bank (1994)).

Table A36. Pakistan, Panama

	1970	1971	1972	1973	1974	1975	1976	1977	1978	1979	1980	1981
Pakistan												
Domestic constraint	—	—	—[1]	—	—	—	—	—	—	—	—	—
Exchange rate regime	BWP	BWP	BWP	UDP	UDP	UDP	UDP	UDP	UDP	UDP	UDP	UDP
Capital controls	N	N	N	N	N	N	N	N	N	N	N	N
IMF program	N	N	Y[2]	Y	Y	Y	N	Y[3]	N	N	N	Y[4]
Panama												
Domestic constraint	FC[5]	FC	FC	FC	FC	FC	FC	FC	FC	FC	FC	FC
Exchange rate regime	UDP[5]	UDP	UDP	UDP	UDP	UDP	UDP	UDP	UDP	UDP	UDP	UDP
Capital controls	N	N	N	N	N	N	N	N	N	N	N	N
IMF program	Y[6]	Y	Y	Y	Y	Y	Y	Y	Y	Y	Y	Y

	1982	1983	1984	1985	1986	1987	1988	1989	1990	1991	1992	1993	1994
Pakistan													
Domestic constraint	—	—	—	—	—	—	—	—	—	—	—	—	—
Exchange rate regime	FL[7]	FL	FL	FL	FL	FL	FL	FL	FL	FL	FL	FL	FL
Capital controls	N	N	N	N	N	N	N	N	N	N	N	N	N
IMF program	Y	Y	Y	N	N	N	N	N	Y[8]	Y	Y	N	Y[9]
Panama													
Domestic constraint	FC	FC	FC	FC	FC	FC	FC	FC	FC	FC	FC	FC	FC
Exchange rate regime	UDP	UDP	UDP	UDP	UDP	UDP	UDP	UDP	UDP	UDP	UDP	UDP	UDP
Capital controls	N	N	N	N	N	N	N	N	N	N	N	N	N
IMF program	Y	Y	Y	Y	Y	N	N	N	N	N	Y[10]	Y	N

[1]As of 1992, the State Credit Consultative Committee under the chairmanship of the Governor of the State Bank of Pakistan prepares annual credit plans based on a broad money target. The targets, however, are not announced ex ante (and are published ex post only occasionally).

[2]May 18, 1972–May 17, 1973; August 11, 1973–August 10, 1974; November 11, 1974–November 10, 1975.

[3]March 9, 1977–March 8, 1978.

[4]November 24, 1980–November 23, 1983.

[5]Except for fractional coins, there is no issue of currency in Panama. The U.S. dollar is used as a legal tender. The balboa is used as a unit of account at a rate of B1 per U.S. dollar.

[6]January 16, 1969–January 15, 1970; February 3, 1970–February 2, 1971; March 23, 1971–March 22, 1972; June 22, 1972–June 21, 1973; August 3, 1973–August 2, 1974; October 16, 1974–October 15, 1975; November 8, 1975–November 7, 1976; April 6, 1977–April 5, 1978; June 9, 1978–June 8, 1979; March 23, 1978–March 22, 1980; April 18, 1980–December 31, 1981; April 28, 1982–April 27, 1983; June 24, 1983–December 31, 1984; July 15, 1985–March 31, 1987.

[7]As of January 8, 1982, the exchange rate has been managed based on a currency basket.

[8]December 28, 1988–December 27, 1991.

[9]September 16, 1993–September 15, 1994.

[10]February 24, 1992–December 23, 1993.

Table A37. Paraguay, Peru

	1970	1971	1972	1973	1974	1975	1976	1977	1978	1979	1980	1981
Paraguay												
Domestic constraint[1]	—	—	—	—	—	—	—	—	—	—	—	—
Exchange rate regime	BW	BW	UDP	UDP	UDP	UDP	UDP	UDP	UDP	UDP	UDP	UDP
Capital controls	Y	Y	Y	Y	Y	Y	Y	Y	Y	Y	Y	Y
IMF program	N	N	N	N	N	N	N	N	N	N	N	N
Peru												
Domestic constraint	—	—	—	—	—	—	—	—	—	—	—	—
Exchange rate regime	UDP	UDP	UDP	UDP	UDP	UDP	FL	FL	FL	FL	FL	FL
Capital controls	Y	Y	Y	Y	Y	Y	Y	Y	N	N	N	N
IMF program	N	N	N	N	N	N	N	N[2]	N	Y[3]	Y	Y

	1982	1983	1984	1985	1986	1987	1988	1989	1990	1991	1992	1993	1994
Paraguay													
Domestic constraint[1]	—	—	—	—	—	—	—	—	—	—	—	—	—
Exchange rate regime	UDP	UDP	UDP	UDP	UDP	UDP	UDP	FL[4]	FL	FL	FL	FL	FL
Capital controls	N	N	Y	Y	Y	Y	Y	Y	Y	Y	Y	Y	Y
IMF program	N	N	N	N	N	N	N	N	N	N	N	N	N
Peru													
Domestic constraint	—	—	—	—	—	—	—	—	—	—	—	—	—
Exchange rate regime	FL	FL	FL	UDP[5]	UDP	UDP	UDP	UDP	FL	FL	FL	FL	FL
Capital controls	N	N	Y	Y	Y	Y	Y	Y	Y	Y	Y	N	N
IMF program	Y[6]	Y	Y	N	N	N	N	N	N	N	Y	Y[7]	Y

[1]Since the 1957 stabilization, the Central Bank of Paraguay prepares an annual monetary program to set the domestic credit expansion of the bank. The targets, however, are not published.

[2]November 1977–suspended in February 1978.

[3]September 1978–September 1979.

[4]In February 1989, the exchange rate was unified and the guaraní floated. During the 1980s, a complex system of multiple exchange rates was in place.

[5]Although formally pegged, the exchange rate was often devalued in 1985–86, and multiple currencies practices were in place.

[6]June 1982–April 1984; May 1984–April 1985.

[7]March 1993–March 1996; this arrangement was preceded (as of September 1991) by a rights accumulation program not involving use of IMF resources.

Table A38. Philippines, Portugal

	1970	1971	1972	1973	1974	1975	1976	1977	1978	1979	1980	1981
Philippines												
Domestic constraint	—	—	—	—	—	—	—	—	—	—	—	—
Exchange rate regime	FL[1]	FL	FL	FL	FL	FL	FL	FL	FL	FL	FL	FL
Capital controls	Y	Y	Y	Y	Y	Y	Y	Y	Y	Y	Y	Y
IMF program	Y[2]	Y	Y	Y	Y	Y	Y	Y	Y	Y	Y	Y
Portugal												
Domestic constraint	—	—	—	—	—	—	—	—	—	—	—	—
Exchange rate regime	BWP	BWP	BWP	TWP	TWP	TWP	FL[3]	FL	TWCP[4]	TWCP	TWCP	TWCP
Capital controls	Y	Y	Y	Y	Y	Y	Y	Y	N	N	N	N
IMF program	N	N	N	N	N	N	N	Y[5]	Y	N	N	N

	1982	1983	1984	1985	1986	1987	1988	1989	1990	1991	1992	1993	1994
Philippines													
Domestic constraint	—	—	—	—	—	—	—	—	—	—	—	—	—
Exchange rate regime	FL	FL	FL	FL[6]	FL	FL	FL	FL	FL	FL	FL	FL	FL
Capital controls	Y	Y	Y	Y	Y	Y	Y	Y	Y	Y	Y	Y	Y
IMF program	N	Y[7]	N	Y[8]	Y	Y	N	Y[9]	Y	Y	Y	N	Y[10]
Portugal													
Domestic constraint	—	—	—	—[11]	—	—	—	—	—	—	—	—	—
Exchange rate regime	TWCP	TWCP	TWCP	TWCP	TWCP	TWCP	TWCP	TWCP	TWCP	FL[12]	ERM[13]	ERM	ERM
Capital controls	N	N	Y	Y	Y	Y	Y	Y	Y	Y	Y	N	N
IMF program	N	N	Y[14]	N	N	N	N	N	N	N	N	N	N

[1]Between 1970 and 1984, the exchange rate was subject to managed float; during this period, it was subject to long periods of stability (e.g., in the second half of the 1970s).

[2]February 20, 1970–February 19, 1971; March 16, 1971–March 15, 1972; March 11, 1972–May 10, 1973; May 16, 1973–May 15, 1974; July 16, 1974–July 15, 1975; May 31, 1975–May 30, 1976; April 2, 1976–April 1, 1979; June 11, 1979–December 31, 1979; February 27, 1980–December 31, 1981.

[3]The exchange rate was often revised (in early 1976 and 1977) through step depreciations; between these step depreciations, the exchange rate was subject to a gradual depreciation, particularly in 1976.

[4]As of August 1977.

[5]April 25, 1977–April 24, 1978; June 5, 1978–June 4, 1979.

[6]Since October 15, 1984, the exchange rate has been determined in the interbank market.

[7]February 25, 1983–February 28, 1984.

[8]December 14, 1984–June 13, 1986; October 24, 1986–April 23, 1988.

[9]May 23, 1989–May 22, 1992; February 20, 1991–August 19, 1992; February 20, 1991–March 31, 1993.

[10]June 24, 1994–June 23, 1997.

[11]During the 1980s, annual targets for broad money aggregate (L-), including treasury bills, were set by the Bank of Portugal but were not announced.

[12]Between October 1990 and April 1991, the exchange rate was floating around a medium-term traded-weighted crawling peg reflecting the inflation differential vis-à-vis five countries.

[13]As of April 1992, with a 6 percent band on each side.

[14]October 7, 1983–February 28, 1985.

Table A39. Saudi Arabia, Senegal

	1970	1971	1972	1973	1974	1975	1976	1977	1978	1979	1980	1981
Saudi Arabia												
Domestic constraint	—	—	—	—	—	—	—	—	—	—	—	—
Exchange rate regime	BW	BW	UDP	UDP	UDP	SDP[1]	SDP	SDP	SDP	SDP	SDP	SDP
Capital controls	N	N	N	N	N	N	N	N	N	N	N	N
IMF program	N	N	N	N	N	N	N	N	N	N	N	N
Senegal												
Domestic constraint	CU	CU	CU	CU	CU	CU	CU	CU	CU	CU	CU	CU
Exchange rate regime	FFP	FFP	FFP	FFP	FFP	FFP	FFP	FFP	FFP	FFP	FFP	FFP
Capital controls	Y	Y	Y	Y	Y	Y	Y	Y	Y	Y	Y	Y
IMF program	N	N	N	N	N	N	N	N	N	Y[2]	Y	Y

	1982	1983	1984	1985	1986	1987	1988	1989	1990	1991	1992	1993	1994
Saudi Arabia													
Domestic constraint	—	—	—	—	—	—	—	—	—	—	—	—	—
Exchange rate regime	SDP	SDP	SDP	SDP	SDP	SDP	SDP	SDP	SDP	SDP	SDP	SDP	SDP
Capital controls	N	N	N	N	N	N	N	N	N	N	N	N	N
IMF program	N	N	N	N	N	N	N	N	N	N	N	N	N
Senegal													
Domestic constraint	CU	CU	CU	CU	CU	CU	CU	CU	CU	CU	CU	CU	CU
Exchange rate regime	FFP	FFP	FFP	FFP	FFP	FFP	FFP	FFP	FFP	FFP	FFP	FFP	FFP
Capital controls	Y	Y	Y	Y	Y	Y	Y	Y	Y	Y	Y	Y	Y
IMF program	Y	Y	Y	Y	Y	Y	Y	Y	Y	Y	N	N	N[3]

[1]Formally the riyal is pegged to the SDR with margins of 7.25 percent on each side; since mid-1991, observance of these margins has been suspended. In practice, the riyal has shown limited flexibility vis-à-vis the U.S. dollar.

[2]March 30, 1978–March 29, 1980; August 8, 1980–August 7, 1983; September 11, 1981–September 10, 1982; November 24, 1982–November 23, 1983; September 19, 1983–September 18, 1984; January 16, 1985–July 15, 1986; November 1, 1986–November 10, 1987; October 26, 1987–October 25, 1988; November 21, 1988–June 2, 1992.

[3]August 29, 1994–August 28, 1997.

Table A40. Singapore, South Africa

	1970	1971	1972	1973	1974	1975	1976	1977	1978	1979	1980	1981
Singapore												
Domestic constraint	CB	—[1]	—	—	—	—	—	—	—	—	—	—
Exchange rate regime	LLP[2]	LLP[2]	UDP[2]	FL[3]	FL	FL	FL	FL	FL	FL	FL[4]	FL
Capital controls	Y	Y	Y	Y	Y	Y	Y	Y	Y	N[5]	N	N
IMF program	N	N	N	N	N	N	N	N	N	N	N	N
South Africa												
Domestic constraint	—	—	—	—	—	—	—	—	—	—	—	—
Exchange rate regime	BWP	BWP	LLP[6]	UDP	FL[7]	UDP	UDP	UDP	UDP	UDP	FL[8]	FL
Capital controls	Y	Y	Y	Y	Y	Y	Y	Y	Y	Y	Y	Y
IMF program	N	N	N	N	N	N	Y[9]	Y	N	N	N	N

	1982	1983	1984	1985	1986	1987	1988	1989	1990	1991	1992	1993	1994
Singapore													
Domestic constraint	—	—	—	—	—	—	—	—	—	—	—	—	—
Exchange rate regime	FL	FL	FL	FL	FL	FL	FL	FL	FL	FL	FL	FL	FL
Capital controls	N	N	N	N	N	N	N	N	N	N	N	N	N
IMF program	N	N	N	N	N	N	N	N	N	N	N	N	N
South Africa													
Domestic constraint	—	—	—	—	BMT[10]	BMT	BMT	BMT	BMT	BMT	BMT	BMT	BMT
Exchange rate regime	FL	FL	FL	FL	FL	FL	FL	FL	FL	FL	FL	FL	FL
Capital controls	Y	Y	Y	Y	Y	Y	Y	Y	Y	Y	Y	Y	Y
IMF program	N	Y[11]	N	N	N	N	N	N	N	N	N	N	N

[1]In 1971, the Monetary Authority of Singapore was set up (Wood (1992)).

[2]Until May 8, 1975, the Singapore dollar was exchanged at par with the Malaysian dollar; the pegging arrangements with other countries were therefore the same (see Table A29).

[3]As of June 20, 1973.

[4]As of 1980, the Monetary Authority of Singapore (MAS) monitors the exchange rate against an undisclosed trade-weighted basket of currencies within a target band. The target depends on the currency and projected inflationary pressure. Wood (1992) finds that the MAS follows a monetary rule.

[5]As of June 1978.

[6]May–September 1972.

[7]In June 1974, a managed float was introduced; the Reserve Bank came close to applying a fixed-basket pegging with changes in the rand-dollar rate effected every few weeks (see Commission of Inquiry into the Monetary System and Monetary Policy in South Africa (1978)); this policy lasted until June 27, 1975.

[8]On January 24, 1979, a flexible exchange rate was introduced. At the same time, a financial rand exchange rate was introduced for certain financial transactions. The dual exchange rate system was temporarily abolished in February 1983–August 1985.

[9]January 21, 1976–January 20, 1977; August 6, 1976–August 5, 1977.

[10]The first targets were announced in the second half of 1985 for the period starting in the last quarter of 1985; the change followed the recommendations of the Commission of Inquiry into the Monetary System and Monetary Policy in South Africa, which recommended to implement monetary targeting with a fair measure of flexibility and with a low profile (see South African Reserve Bank (1986)). In recent years, the term "guidelines" has replaced the term "target."

[11]November 3, 1982–December 31, 1983.

Table A41. Spain, Sri Lanka

	1970	1971	1972	1973	1974	1975	1976	1977	1978	1979	1980	1981
Spain												
Domestic constraint	—	—	—	—[1]	—	—	—	—	BMT	BMT	BMT	BMT
Exchange rate regime	BWP	BWP	BWP	BWP	TWP[2]	TWP	TWP	TWP	FL	FL	FL	FL
Capital controls	Y	Y	Y	Y	Y	Y	Y	Y	Y	Y	Y	Y
IMF program	N	N	N	N	N	N	N	N	Y[3]	N	N	N
Sri Lanka												
Domestic constraint	—	—	—	—	—	—	—	—	—	—	—	—[4]
Exchange rate regime	BWP	BWP	LLP[5]	LLP	LLP	LLP	LLP	FL[6]	FL	FL	FL	FL
Capital controls	Y	Y	Y	Y	Y	Y	Y	Y	Y	Y	Y	Y
IMF program	Y[7]	Y	N	N	Y[8]	N	N	N	Y[9]	Y	Y	Y

	1982	1983	1984	1985	1986	1987	1988	1989	1990	1991	1992	1993	1994
Spain													
Domestic constraint	BMT	BMT	BMT	BMT	BMT	BMT	BMT	BMT	BMT	BMT	BMT	BMT	BMT[10]
Exchange rate regime	FL	FL	FL	FL	FL	FL	FL	ERM[11]	ERM	ERM	ERM	EMR	ERM
Capital controls	Y	Y	Y	Y	Y	Y	Y	Y	Y	Y	Y	N	N
IMF program	N	N	N	N	N	N	N	N	N	N	N	N	N
Sri Lanka													
Domestic constraint	—	—	—	—	—	—	—	—	—	—	—	—	—
Exchange rate regime	FL	FL	FL	FL	FL	FL	FL	FL	FL	FL	FL	FL	FL
Capital controls	Y	Y	Y[12]	Y	Y	Y	Y	Y	Y	Y	Y	Y	Y
IMF program	N	N	Y[12]	N	N	N	Y[13]	Y	Y	Y	Y	Y	Y

[1]The Bank of Spain started setting targets for broad money in 1973; targets started to be announced in 1978.

[2]As of January 22, 1974.

[3]February 6, 1978–February 5, 1979.

[4]Starting in 1981, the central bank prepared "credit plans" that were used as a basis for setting bank-by-bank credit ceilings; the credit plans were based on "monetary surveys" involving projections for broad money growth. These projections, however, were not made public.

[5]As of May 9, 1972.

[6]A more flexible exchange rate policy, based on a managed float, was introduced. In practice, since 1980, the rupee real effective exchange rate closely followed the movements of the U.S. dollar real effective exchange rate.

[7]August 12, 1969–August 11, 1970; March 18, 1971–March 17, 1972.

[8]April 30, 1974–April 29, 1975.

[9]December 2, 1977–December 1, 1978; January 1, 1979–December 31, 1981.

[10]A new monetary framework based on inflation targeting was announced in early 1995.

[11]As of June 1989, with a 6 percent band on both sides.

[12]September 14, 1983–July 31, 1984.

[13]March 14, 1988–March 13, 1991; September 13, 1991–March 29, 1995.

Table A42. Swaziland, Sweden

	1970	1971	1972	1973	1974	1975	1976	1977	1978	1979	1980	1981
Swaziland												
Domestic constraint	FC[1]	FC	FC	FC	CB[2]	CB	CB	CB	CB	CB	CB	CB
Exchange rate regime	SRP[1]	SRP	SRP	SRP	SRP	SRP	SRP	SRP	SRP	SRP	SRP	SRP
Capital controls	N	N	N	N	N	N	N	N	N	N	N	N
IMF program	N	N	N	N	N	N	N	N	N	N	N	N
Sweden												
Domestic constraint	—	—	—	—	—	—	—	—	—	—	—	—
Exchange rate regime	BWP	BWP	ECM	ECM	ECM	ECM	ECM	ECM	TWP[3]	TWP	TWP	TWP
Capital controls	Y	Y	Y	Y	Y	Y	Y	Y	Y	Y	Y	Y
IMF program												

	1982	1983	1984	1985	1986	1987	1988	1989	1990	1991	1992	1993	1994
Swaziland													
Domestic constraint	CB	CB	CB	CB	CB	CB	CB	CB	CB	CB	CB	CB	CB
Exchange rate regime	SRP	SRP	SRP	SRP	SRP[4]	SRP	SRP	SRP	SRP	SRP	SRP	SRP	SRP
Capital controls	N	N	N	N	N	N	N	N	N	N	N	N	N
IMF program	N	N	N	N	N	N	N	N	N	N	N	N	N
Sweden													
Domestic constraint	—	—	—	—	—	—	—	—	—	—	—	IT	IT[5]
Exchange rate regime	TWP	TWP	TWP	TWP	TWP	TWP	TWP	TWP	TWP	EUP[6]	EUP	FL[7]	FL
Capital controls	Y	Y	Y	Y	Y	Y	Y	Y	Y	Y	Y	N	N
IMF program													

[1]The South African rand was the sole legal tender until 1974. On April 1, 1974, the Monetary Authority of Swaziland (Central Bank of Swaziland as of 1979) was established and a domestic currency (lilangeni) was introduced. The rand remained legal tender until mid-1986.

[2]All currency issues must be backed by reserves in rand; as of 1986, part of the reserves can be held in convertible currencies.

[3]As of August 1977.

[4]As of April 1, 1986, the parity with the rand can be altered.

[5]Inflation targets first announced on January 15, 1993.

[6]As of May 1991.

[7]As of November 1992.

Table A43. Switzerland, Taiwan Province of China

	1970	1971	1972	1973	1974	1975	1976	1977	1978	1979	1980	1981
Switzerland												
Domestic constraint	—	—	—	—	—	NMT	NMT	NMT	NMT[1]	—	HMT	HMT
Exchange rate regime	UDP	UDP	UDP	FL	FL	FL	FL	FL	FL	DMP	FL	FL
Capital controls	N	N	N	N	N	N	N	N	N	N	N	N
IMF program	N	N	N	N	N	N	N	N	N	N	N	N
Taiwan Province of China												
Domestic constraint	—	—	—	—	—	—	—	—	—	—	—	—
Exchange rate regime	UDP[2]	UDP	UDP	UDP	UDP	UDP	UDP	UDP	UDP	UDP	UDP	UDP
Capital controls	Y	Y	Y	Y	Y	Y	Y	Y	Y	Y	Y	Y
IMF program	N	N	N	N	N	N	N	N	N	N	N	N

	1982	1983	1984	1985	1986	1987	1988	1989	1990	1991	1992	1993	1994
Switzerland													
Domestic constraint	HMT	HMT	HMT	HMT	HMT	HMT	HMT	HMT	HMT[3]	HMT	HMT	HMT	HMT
Exchange rate regime	FL	FL	FL	FL	FL	FL	FL	FL	FL	FL	FL	FL	FL
Capital controls	N	N	N	N	N	N	N	N	N	N	N	N	N
IMF program	N	N	N	N	N	N	N	N	N	N	N	N	N
Taiwan Province of China													
Domestic constraint	—	—	—	—	—	—	—	—	—	—	—	—	—
Exchange rate regime	UDP	UDP	UDP	UDP	FL	FL	FL	FL	FL	FL	FL	FL	FL
Capital controls	Y	Y	Y	Y	Y	Y	Y	Y	Y	Y	Y	Y	Y
IMF program	N	N	N	N	N	N	N	N	N	N	N	N	N

[1]Abandoned in the fall of 1978 (Rich (1991)).
[2]Between 1961 and 1985, the exchange rate was de facto pegged to the U.S. dollar.
[3]A medium-term framework for monetary targeting was introduced at the end of 1990, with less reliance on short-term volatility of money.

Table A44. Thailand, Togo

	1970	1971	1972	1973	1974	1975	1976	1977	1978	1979	1980	1981
Thailand												
Domestic constraint	—	—	—	—	—	—	—	—	—	—	—	—
Exchange rate regime	UDP	UDP	UDP	UDP[1]	UDP	UDP	UDP	UDP	TWP[2]	TWP	TWP	TWP
Capital controls	Y	Y	Y	Y	Y	Y	Y	Y	Y	Y	Y	Y
IMF program	N	N	N	N	N	N	N	N	Y[3]	N	N	Y[4]
Togo												
Domestic constraint	CU	CU	CU	CU	CU	CU	CU	CU	CU	CU	CU	CUA
Exchange rate regime	FFP	FFP	FFP	FFP	FFP	FFP	FFP	FFP	FFP	FFP	FFP	FFP
Capital controls	Y	Y	Y	Y	Y	Y	Y	Y	Y	Y	Y	Y
IMF program	N	N	N	N	N	N	N	N	N	Y[5]	N	N

	1982	1983	1984	1985	1986	1987	1988	1989	1990	1991	1992	1993	1994
Thailand													
Domestic constraint	—	—	—	—	—	—	—	—	—	—	—	—	—
Exchange rate regime	UDP[6]	UDP	UDP	TWP[7]	TWP	TWP	TWP	TWP	TWP	TWP	TWP	TWP	TWP
Capital controls	Y	Y	Y	Y	Y	Y	Y	Y	Y	Y	Y	Y	Y
IMF program	Y	Y	N	Y[8]	Y	Y	N	N	N	N	N	N	N
Togo													
Domestic constraint	CU	CU	CU	CU	CU	CU	CU	CU	CU	CU	CU	CU	CU
Exchange rate regime	FFP	FFP	FFP	FFP	FFP	FFP	FFP	FFP	FFP	FFP	FFP	FFP	FFP
Capital controls	Y	Y	Y	Y	Y	Y	Y	Y	Y	Y	Y	Y	Y
IMF program	N	N	N	N	N	N	N	N	N	N	N	N	N[9]

[1]On July 15, 1973, the wider margin of 2.25 percent (instead of the original 1 percent) was introduced.
[2]Introduced on March 8, 1978.
[3]July 1, 1978–June 30, 1979.
[4]June 31, 1981–March 31, 1983; and November 17, 1982–December 31, 1983.
[5]June 11, 1979–December 31, 1980; February 13, 1981–February 11, 1983; March 4, 1983–April 3, 1984; May 7, 1984–May 6, 1985; May 17, 1985–May 16, 1986; June 2, 1986–April 18, 1988; March 31, 1988–May 19, 1993.
[6]As of July 15, 1981.
[7]As of November 1984.
[8]June 14, 1985–December 31, 1987.
[9]September 16, 1994–September 16, 1997.

Table A45. Trinidad and Tobago, Tunisia

	1970	1971	1972	1973	1974	1975	1976	1977	1978	1979	1980	1981
Trinidad and Tobago												
Domestic constraint	—	—	—	—	—	—	—	—	—	—	—	—
Exchange rate regime	BWP	BWP	LLP[1]	LLP	LLP	LLP	UDP	UDP	UDP	UDP	UDP	UDP
Capital controls	Y	Y	Y	Y	Y	Y	Y	Y	Y	Y	Y	Y
IMF program	N	N	N	N	N	N	N	N	N	N	N	N
Tunisia												
Domestic constraint	—	—	—	—	—	—	—	—	—	—	—	—
Exchange rate regime	BWP	BWP	BWP	FL[2]	FL	FL	FL	FL	FL	FL	FL	FL
Capital controls	Y	Y	Y	Y	Y	Y	Y	Y	Y	Y	Y	Y
IMF program	Y[3]	N	N	N	N	N	N	N	N	N	N	N

	1982	1983	1984	1985	1986	1987	1988	1989	1990	1991	1992	1993	1994
Trinidad and Tobago													
Domestic constraint	—	—	—	—	—	—	—	—	—	—	—	—	—
Exchange rate regime	UDP	UDP	UDP	UDP	UDP	UDP	UDP	UDP	UDP	UDP	UDP	FL[4]	FL
Capital controls	Y	Y	Y	Y	Y	Y	Y	Y	Y	Y	Y	Y	Y
IMF program	N	N	N	N	N	N	N	Y[5]	Y	N	N	N	N
Tunisia													
Domestic constraint	—	—	—	—	—	—	—	—	—	—	—	—	—
Exchange rate regime	FL	FL	FL	FL	FL	FL	FL	FL	FL	FL	FL	FL	FL
Capital controls	Y	Y	Y	Y	Y	Y	Y	Y	Y	Y	Y	Y	Y
IMF program	N	N	N	N	N	Y[6]	Y	Y	Y	Y	Y	N	N

[1]As of May 9, 1972.

[2]The dinar was officially floating during 1973–77. It was pegged to a currency basket in 1978–87. It was subject to managed float thereafter. Frequent depreciations took place in 1978–87, although by less than needed to maintain competitiveness.

[3]January 1, 1970–December 31, 1970.

[4]As of April 13, 1993.

[5]January 13, 1989–February 28, 1990; April 20, 1990–March 31, 1991.

[6]November 5, 1986–May 3, 1988; July 25, 1988–July 24, 1992.

Table A46. Turkey, Uganda

	1970	1971	1972	1973	1974	1975	1976	1977	1978	1979	1980	1981
Turkey												
Domestic constraint	—	—	—	—	—	—	—	—	—	—	—	—
Exchange rate regime	BWP	BWP	BWP	FL	FL	FL	FL	FL	FL	FL	FL	FL
Capital controls	Y	Y	Y	Y	Y	Y	Y	Y	Y	Y	Y	Y
IMF program	Y[1]	Y	N	N	N	N	N	N	Y[2]	Y	Y	Y
Uganda												
Domestic constraint	—	—	—	—	—	—	—	—	—	—	—	—
Exchange rate regime	BWP	BWP	UDP	UDP	UDP	UDP	SDP	SDP	SDP	SDP	SDP	FL[3]
Capital controls	Y	Y	Y	Y	Y	Y	Y	Y	Y	Y	Y	Y
IMF program	N	N	Y[4]	N	N	N	N	N	N	N	Y[5]	Y

	1982	1983	1984	1985	1986	1987	1988	1989	1990	1991	1992	1993	1994
Turkey													
Domestic constraint	—	—	—	—	—[6]	—	—	—	BMT[7]	BMT	BMT	—	—
Exchange rate regime	FL	FL	FL	FL	FL	FL	FL	FL	FL	FL	FL	FL	FL
Capital controls	Y	Y	Y	Y	Y	Y	Y	Y	Y	Y	Y	Y	Y
IMF program	Y	Y	Y	N	N	N	N	N	N	N	N	N	N[8]
Uganda													
Domestic constraint	—	—	—	—	—	—	—	—	—	—	—	—	—
Exchange rate regime	FL	FL	FL	FL	FL	FL	FL	FL	FL	FL	FL	FL	FL
Capital controls	Y	Y	Y	N	Y	Y	Y	Y	Y	Y	Y	Y	Y
IMF program	Y	Y	Y	N	N	Y[9]	Y	Y	Y	Y	Y	Y[9]	Y

[1]July 1, 1969–June 30, 1970; August 17, 1970–August 16, 1971.

[2]April 24, 1978–April 23, 1980; July 19, 1979–July 18, 1980; June 18, 1980–June 17, 1983; June 24, 1983–June 23, 1984; April 4, 1984–April 3, 1985.

[3]As of May 1981; between 1987 and September 1990, the shilling was formally pegged to the U.S. dollar but was subject to frequent revisions in order to maintain competitiveness; between October 1990 and March 1992, the shilling was formally pegged to a currency basket with frequent depreciations; as of April 1992, the exchange rate was determined in auctions; as of November 1993, it was determined in an interbank market.

[4]July 22, 1971–July 21, 1972.

[5]January 4, 1980–December 1980; June 5, 1981–June 30, 1982; August 11, 1982–August 10, 1983; September 16, 1983–September 15, 1984.

[6]Unannounced targets were set for broad money during 1986–88.

[7]As of January 1990; in addition, subtargets were announced for other aggregates of the central bank balance sheet.

[8]July 8, 1994–September 7, 1995.

[9]June 15, 1987–June 4, 1990; April 17, 1989–November 24, 1993; September 6, 1994–September 5, 1997.

Table A47. United Kingdom, United States

	1970	1971	1972	1973	1974	1975	1976	1977	1978	1979	1980	1981
United Kingdom												
Domestic constraint	—	—	—	—	—	—	—	BMT[1]	BMT	BMT[2]	BMT	BMT
Exchange rate regime	BW	BW	FL[3]	FL	FL	FL	FL	FL	FL	FL	FL	FL
Capital controls	Y	Y	Y	Y	Y	Y	Y	Y	Y	N	N	N
IMF program	N[4]	N	N	N	N	N	Y[5]	Y	Y	N	N	N
United States												
Domestic constraint	—[6]	—	—	—	—	NMT[7]	NMT	NMT	NMT[8]	NMT	NMT	NMT
Exchange rate regime	FL	FL	FL	FL	FL	FL	FL	FL	FL	FL	FL	FL
Capital controls	N	N	N	N	N	N	N	N	N	N	N	N
IMF program	N	N	N	N	N	N	N	N	N	N	N	N

	1982	1983	1984	1985	1986	1987	1988	1989	1990	1991	1992	1993	1994
United Kingdom													
Domestic constraint	BMT	HMT[9]	HMT	HMT	HMT	HMT	HMT	HMT	HMT	HMT	HMT	IT[10]	IT
Exchange rate regime	FL	FL	FL	FL	FL	DMP[11]	FL	FL	FL	ERM[12]	ERM	FL	FL
Capital controls	N	N	N	N	N	N	N	N	N	N	N	N	N
IMF program	N	N	N	N	N	N	N	N	N	N	N	N	N
United States													
Domestic constraint	NMT	NMT	NMT	NMT	NMT	NMT	BMT	BMT	BMT	BMT	BMT	—[13]	—
Exchange rate regime	FL	FL	FL	FL	FL	FL	FL	FL	FL	FL	FL	FL	FL
Capital controls	N	N	N	N	N	N	N	N	N	N	N	N	N
IMF program	N	N	N	N	N	N	N	N	N	N	N	N	N

[1]Set in July 1976 for 1976–77.

[2]The medium-term financial strategy introduced targets for the forthcoming four years; as of 1981, the figures announced beyond the first year were announced as "illustrative ranges" (Townend (1991)).

[3]During May–June 1972, the pound joined the European Common Margin Arrangement.

[4]June 29, 1969–June 19, 1970.

[5]December 31, 1975–December 30, 1976; January 3, 1977–January 2, 1979.

[6]In the early 1970s, the Federal Open Market Committee (FOMC) started including money growth rates in the monthly policy directives to the trading desk (Friedman (1982)).

[7]As of May 1975, targets were announced for M1 following House Concurrent Resolution 133 of March 1975.

[8]Humphrey-Hawkins Act.

[9]As of 1984, the authorities started announcing, in addition to the broad money target announced until then (sterling M3), also targets for M0 (basically, currency in circulation). As of 1987, the sterling M3 target was dropped.

[10]Letter by the Chancellor to the Treasury Civil Service Committee of the House of Commons (October 8, 1992); the M0 target was formally retained.

[11]For one year from March 1987, the exchange rate against the DM was not allowed to rise above DM3 (Townend (1991)).

[12]As of October 1990, with a 6 percent band on both sides.

[13]On February 19, 1993, Chairman Greenspan announced that the Federal Reserve was giving "less weight to monetary aggregates as guides to policy" (Greenspan (1993)).

Table A48. Uruguay, Venezuela

	1970	1971	1972	1973	1974	1975	1976	1977	1978	1979	1980	1981
Uruguay												
Domestic constraint	NMT	NMT	NMT	NMT	—	—	—	—	—	—	—	—
Exchange rate regime	UDP	UDP	FL[1]	FL	FL	FL	FL	FL	FL	UDCP[2]	UDCP	UDCP
Capital controls	Y	Y	Y	Y	Y	N[3]	N	N	N	N	N	N
IMF program	Y[4]	N	Y[5]	N	N	Y[6]	Y	Y	Y	Y	Y	Y
Venezuela												
Domestic constraint	—	—	—	—	—	—	—	—	—	—	—	—
Exchange rate regime	UDP	UDP	UDP	UDP	UDP	UDP	UDP	UDP	UDP	UDP	UDP	UDP
Capital controls	N	N	N	N	N	N	N	N	N	N	N	N
IMF program	N	N	N	N	N	N	N	N	N	N	N	N

	1982	1983	1984	1985	1986	1987	1988	1989	1990	1991	1992	1993	1994
Uruguay													
Domestic constraint	—	—	—	—	NMT[7]	BMT	BMT	BMT	—	—	—	—	—
Exchange rate regime	UDCP	FL[8]	FL	FL	FL	FL	FL	FL	FL	FL	UDCP[9]	UDCP	UDCP
Capital controls	N	N	N	N	N	N	N	N	N	N	N	N	N
IMF program	Y	Y	Y	Y	Y	N[10]	N	N	N	Y[11]	Y	Y	N[12]
Venezuela													
Domestic constraint	—	—	—	—	—	—	—	—	—	—	—	—	—
Exchange rate regime	UDP	FL[13]	FL	FL	FL	FL	FL	FL[14]	FL	FL	FL	FL	UDP[15]
Capital controls	N	Y	Y	Y	Y	Y	Y	Y	Y	Y	Y	Y	Y
IMF program	N	N	N	N	N	N	Y[16]	Y	Y	Y	Y	N	N

[1]From March 1972, a floating exchange rate was used for financial transactions, and a crawling peg (adjusted in line within inflation) was used for commercial transactions. The crawling peg was unified in 1975.

[2]Between November 1978 and November 1982, the exchange rate was gradually depreciated according to a "tablita," which was announced several months in advance.

[3]Capital controls were lifted in September 1974.

[4]May 28, 1970–May 27, 1971.

[5]June 27, 1972–June 26, 1973.

[6]May 9, 1975–May 8, 1976; August 4, 1976–August 3, 1977; September 14, 1977–September 13, 1978; March 19, 1979–March 15, 1980; May 14, 1980–May 13, 1981; July 15, 1981–July 14, 1982; April 22, 1983–April 29, 1985; September 27, 1985–March 26, 1987.

[7]Targets were set annually for each financial year. In 1986, targets were announced also for base money and broad money.

[8]Between December 1982 and 1985, the exchange rate floated. As of 1985, the central bank announces periodically its intervention rates.

[9]Since 1992, the reference exchange rate around which the peso is allowed to float has been depreciated by 2 percent a month, in line with targeted inflation.

[10]Procedure for enhanced surveillance based on the monitoring of a "shadow program" between July 1987 and end-1989.

[11]December 12, 1990–March 15, 1992; July 1, 1992–June 30, 1994.

[12]Enhanced procedure based on a "shadow program."

[13]In February 1993, a multiple exchange rate system was introduced including two fixed exchange rates—which were, however, frequently depreciated—and a floating rate.

[14]In March 14, 1989, the exchange rate system was unified and the exchange rate was floated; in 1992, intervention increased and in April 1993, a de facto crawling peg was adopted and the bolivar started depreciating by BS 0.10–0.15 per U.S. dollar per day. On May 4, 1994, an auction system was introduced.

[15]On June 27, 1994, a fixed exchange rate of BS 170 per U.S. dollar was introduced.

[16]June 23, 1989–March 22, 1993.

Table A49. WAMU (West African Monetary Union), Western Samoa

	1970	1971	1972	1973	1974	1975	1976	1977	1978	1979	1980	1981
WAMU[1]												
Domestic constraint	—	—	—	—	—	—[2]	—	—	—	—	—	—
Exchange rate regime	FFP	FFP	FFP	FFP	FFP	FFP	FFP	FFP	FFP	FFP	FFP	FFP
Capital controls	Y	Y	Y	Y	Y	Y	Y	Y	Y	Y	Y	Y
IMF program	N	N	N	N	N	N	N	N	N	N	N	N
Western Samoa												
Domestic constraint	—	—	—	—	—	—	—	—	—	—	—	—
Exchange rate regime	BWP	BWP	BWP	UDP	UDP	UDP	FL[3]	FL	FL	FL	FL	FL
Capital controls	Y	Y	Y	Y	Y	Y	Y	Y	Y	Y	Y	Y
IMF program	N	N	N	N	N	N	N	Y[4]	Y	Y	Y	N

	1982	1983	1984	1985	1986	1987	1988	1989	1990	1991	1992	1993	1994
WAMU[1]													
Domestic constraint	—	—	—	—	—	—	—	—	—	—	—	—	—
Exchange rate regime	FFP	FFP	FFP	FFP	FFP	FFP	FFP	FFP	FFP	FFP	FFP	FFP	FFP
Capital controls	Y	Y	Y	Y	Y	Y	Y	Y	Y	Y	Y	Y	Y
IMF program	N	N	N	N	N	N	N	N	N	N	N	N	N
Western Samoa													
Domestic constraint	—	—	—	—	—	—	—	—	—	—	—	—	—
Exchange rate regime	FL	FL	FL	FL	FL	FL	FL	FL	FL	FL	FL	FL	FL
Capital controls	Y	Y	Y	Y	Y	Y	Y	Y	Y	Y	Y	Y	Y
IMF program	N	Y[5]	Y	Y	N	N	N	N	N	N	N	N	N

[1]Including Benin, Burkina Faso, Côte d'Ivoire, Niger, Senegal, and Togo; Mali joined in 1984.

[2]As of 1975, the BCEAO (Central Bank of West African States—the Central Bank of WAMU) initiated the setting of annual targets for monetary aggregates; these targets, however, are not publicly announced.

[3]The exchange rate started being adjusted to maintain competitiveness with reference to a currency basket.

[4]November 12, 1975–November 11, 1976; January 31, 1977–January 30, 1978; February 6, 1978–February 5, 1979; August 17, 1979–August 16, 1980.

[5]June 27, 1983–June 26, 1984; July 2, 1984–July 8, 1985.

Table A50. Zaïre (Democratic Republic of the Congo),[1] Zambia

	1970	1971	1972	1973	1974	1975	1976	1977	1978	1979	1980	1981
Zaïre												
Domestic constraint	—	—	—	—	—	—	—	—	—	—	—	—
Exchange rate regime	BWP	BWP	BWP	UDP	UDP	UDP	SDP[2]	SDP	SDP	FL[3]	FL	FL
Capital controls	Y	Y	Y	Y	Y	Y	Y	Y	Y	Y	Y	Y
IMF program	N	N	N	N	N	N	Y[4]	Y	N	N	Y[5]	Y
Zambia												
Domestic constraint	—	—	—	—	—	—	—	—	—	—	—	—
Exchange rate regime	UDP	UDP	UDP	UDP	UDP	UDP	UDP	SDP[6]	SDP	SDP	SDP	SDP
Capital controls	Y	Y	Y	Y	Y	Y	Y	Y	Y	Y	Y	Y
IMF program	N	N	N	Y[7]	N	N	N	Y[8]	Y	Y	N	Y[9]

	1982	1983	1984	1985	1986	1987	1988	1989	1990	1991	1992	1993	1994
Zaïre													
Domestic constraint	—	—	—	—	—	—	—	—	—	—	—	—	—
Exchange rate regime	FL	FL	FL	FL	FL	FL	FL	FL	FL	FL	FL	FL	FL
Capital controls	Y	Y	Y	Y	Y	Y	Y	Y	Y	Y	Y	Y	Y
IMF program	Y	Y	Y	Y	Y	Y	Y	Y	N	N	N	N	N
Zambia													
Domestic constraint	—	—	—	—	—	—	—	—	—[10]	—	—	—	—
Exchange rate regime	SDP	SDP	CBP[11]	CBP	FL[12]	FL	UDP[13]	FL[14]	FL	FL	FL	FL	FL
Capital controls	Y	Y	Y	Y	Y	Y	Y	Y	Y	Y	Y	Y	Y
IMF program	Y	Y	Y	Y	Y	Y	N	N	N	N	Y[15]	Y	Y

[1]The official name of Zaïre was changed to Democratic Republic of the Congo on May 17, 1997.

[2]As of March 12, 1976.

[3]Starting in November 1978, the exchange rate parity was frequently revised by large amounts. However, a floating exchange rate system was formally introduced only in 1983.

[4]March 22, 1976–March 21, 1977; April 25, 1977–April 24, 1978.

[5]August 27, 1980–February 26, 1981; June 22, 1981–June 22, 1984; December 27, 1983–March 26, 1985; April 24, 1985–April 23, 1986; May 28, 1986–March 27, 1988; May 15, 1987–May 14, 1990.

[6]As of July 9, 1976.

[7]May 4, 1973–May 3, 1974.

[8]July 30, 1976–July 28, 1977; April 26, 1978–April 25, 1980.

[9]May 8, 1981–May 7, 1984; April 18, 1983–April 17, 1984; July 26, 1984–April 10, 1986; February 21, 1986–February 28, 1988.

[10]Broad money targets started being used by the central bank for internal purposes.

[11]As of July 1983.

[12]The exchange rate was floated as of October 15, 1985.

[13]A dollar peg was introduced in 1987; during 1989, the exchange rate started being pegged to the SDR.

[14]Following the June 1989 step devaluation, the kwacha started being frequently devalued; during 1993, a floating exchange rate was formally introduced.

[15]An IMF-monitored program was in place in 1991; a right accommodation program has been in place since July 1992.

References

Aaltonen, Ari, Esko Aurikko, and Jarmo Kontulainen, 1994, *Monetary Policy in Finland* (Helsinki: Bank of Finland).

Aghevli, Bijan B., 1982, "Exchange Rate Policies of Selected Asian Countries," *Finance and Development,* Vol. 19, No. 2 (June), pp. 39–42.

———, and Jorge Márquez-Ruarte, 1985, *A Case of Successful Adjustment: Korea's Experience During 1980–84,* IMF Occasional Paper No. 39 (Washington: International Monetary Fund).

Aghevli, Bijan B., Mohsin S. Khan, and Peter J. Montiel, 1991, *Exchange Rate Policy in Developing Countries: Some Analytical Issues,* IMF Occasional Paper No. 78 (Washington: International Monetary Fund).

Aghevli, Bijan B., Mohsin S. Khan, P. R. Narvekar, and Brock K. Short, 1979, "Monetary Policy in Selected Countries," *Staff Papers,* International Monetary Fund, Vol. 26 (December), pp. 775–824.

Åkerholm, Johnny, and Anne Brunila, 1995, "Inflation Targeting: The Finnish Experience," in *Inflation Targets,* ed. by Leonardo Leiderman and Lars E.O. Svensson (London: Centre for Economic Policy Research).

Alesina, Alberto, Vittorio Grilli, and Gian Maria Milesi-Ferretti, 1993, *The Political Economy of Capital Controls,* CEPR Working Paper No. 793 (London: Centre for Economic Policy Research, June).

Alesina, Alberto, and Lawrence H. Summers, 1993, "Central Bank Independence and Macroeconomic Performance: Some Comparative Evidence," *Journal of Money, Credit and Banking,* Vol. 25 (May), pp. 151–62.

Ammer, John, and Richard T. Freeman, 1995, "Inflation Targeting in the 1990s: The Experiences of New Zealand, Canada, and the United Kingdom," *Journal of Economics and Business,* Vol. 47, No. 2, pp. 165–92.

Amoako, Kingsley Y., 1980, *Balance of Payments and Exchange Rate Policy: The Ghanian Experience* (New York: Garland).

Anayiotos, George C., 1994, "Information Asymmetries in Developing Country Financing," IMF Working Paper No. 94/79 (Washington: International Monetary Fund).

Argy, Victor, Anthony Brennan, and Glenn Stevens, 1990, "Monetary Targeting: The International Experience," *The Economic Record* (March), Vol. 66, pp. 37–62.

Athukorala, Premachandra, and Sirira Jayasuriya, 1994, *Macroeconomic Policies, Crises, and Growth in Sri Lanka, 1969–90* (Washington: World Bank).

Baffi, Paolo, 1989, *Two Aspects of the EMS Negotiations: The Wide Band and the Participation of the United Kingdom in The European Monetary System Ten Years After Its Creation: Results and Prospects* (Rome: Instituto Mobiliare Italiano).

Baliño, Tomás J. T., and Carlo Cottarelli, 1994, "Introduction," in *Frameworks for Monetary Stability—Policy Issues and Country Experiences,* ed. by Tomás J. T. Baliño and Carlo Cottarelli (Washington: International Monetary Fund).

Bank of Botswana, 1985, "Bank of Botswana Tenth Anniversary, 1975–1985" (Gaborone: Bank of Botswana, July).

Bank of Chile, 1992, *Annual Report on 1991* (Santiago).

Bank Negara Malaysia, 1994, *Money and Banking in Malaysia* (Kuala Lumpur).

Bank of Thailand, 1992, *50 Years of the Bank of Thailand: 1942–1992* (Bangkok: Bank of Thailand).

Barro, Robert, and David Gordon, 1983, "Rules, Discretion, and Reputation in a Model of Monetary Policy," *Journal of Monetary Economics,* Vol. 12 (June), pp. 101–22.

———, 1983, "A Positive Theory of Monetary Policy in a Natural Rate Model," *Journal of Political Economy,* Vol. 91 (August), pp. 589–610.

Bartolini, Leonardo, and Allan Drazen, 1995, *Liberalization as News: Can More Be Less?* (unpublished; Washington).

Bean, Charles R., 1992, "Economic and Monetary Union in Europe," *Journal of Economic Perspectives,* Vol. 6 (Fall), pp. 31–52.

Begg, David K. H., 1996, "Monetary Policy in Central and Eastern Europe: Lessons After Half a Decade of Transition," IMF Working Paper No. 96/108 (Washington: International Monetary Fund).

Bercuson, Kenneth, ed., 1995, *Singapore: A Case Study in Rapid Development,* IMF Occasional Paper No. 119 (Washington: International Monetary Fund).

Bernanke, Ben, and Frederic Mishkin, 1992, "Central Bank Behavior and the Strategy of Monetary Policy: Observations from Six Industrialized Countries," NBER Working Paper 4082 (Cambridge, Massachusetts: National Bureau of Economic Research).

Bhatia, Rattan J., 1985, *The West African Monetary Union: An Analytical Review,* IMF Occasional Paper No. 35 (Washington: International Monetary Fund).

Blackburn, Keith, and Michael Christensen, 1989, "Monetary Policy and Policy Credibility: Theories and Evidence," *Journal of Economic Literature,* Vol. 27, No. 1, pp. 1–45.

Blundell-Wignall, Adrian, and Robert G. Gregory, 1990, "Exchange Rate Policy in Advanced Commodity-Exporting Countries: Australia and New Zealand," in *Choosing an Exchange Rate Regime: The Challenge for Smaller Industrial Countries*, ed. by Victor Argy and Paul De Grauwe (Washington: International Monetary Fund).

Bordo, M.D. and B. Eichengreen, 1993, "The Bretton Woods International Monetary System: A Historical Overview," in *A Retrospective on the Bretton Woods System*, ed. by Michael D. Bordo and Barry Eichengreen (Chicago: University of Chicago Press).

Bosman, Hans W.J., 1984, *Monetary Policy in the Netherlands in the Post-Smithsonian Era*, No. 43A, pp.1–23 (Netherlands: Société universitaire européenne de recherches financières).

Boulding, K.E., 1991, "The Legitimacy of Central Banks," *Reappraisal of the Federal Reserve Discount Mechanism* (Washington).

Brekk, Odd Per, 1987, *Norwegian Foreign Exchange Policy*, Skrift series, No. 16 (Norway: Norges Bank), pp. 1–48.

Briault, Clive, Andrew Haldane, and Mervyn King, 1996, "Independence and Accountability," Bank of England Working Paper Series No. 49 (London: Bank of England), pp. 1–49.

Brown, G. Arthur, 1991, "Jamaica's Transition from Direct to Indirect Instruments of Monetary Policy," *The Evolving Role of Central Banks*, ed. by Patrick Downes and Reza Vaez-Zadeh (Washington: International Monetary Fund).

Bruno, Michael, 1991, "Introduction and Overview," in *Lessons of Economic Stabilization and Its Aftermath*, ed. by Michael Bruno, Stanley Fischer, Elhanan Helpman, and Nissan Liviatan (Cambridge, Massachusetts: MIT Press).

———, and Jeffrey D. Sachs, 1985, *Economics of Worldwide Stagflation* (Oxford: Basil Blackwell).

Bryant, Ralph C., 1994, "Comment on André Icard: Monetary Policy and Exchange Rates: The French Experience," in *A Framework for Monetary Stability*, ed. by J.A.H. de Beaufort Wijnholds, S.C.W. Eijffinger, and L.H. Hoogduin (Dordrecht, Netherlands: Kluwer Academic Publishers).

Bufman, Gil, Leonardo Leiderman, and Meir Sokoler, 1994, *Israel's Experience with Explicit Inflation Targets: A First Assessment*, paper presented at the CEPR Workshop on Inflation Targets, Milan, November.

Buiter, Willem H., and Marcus Miller, 1991, "The Thatcher Experiment: The First Two Years," in *Monetary Regime Transformations*, ed. by Barry J. Eichengreen (Aldershot: Edward Elgar).

Burns, Arthur F., 1987, "The Anguish of Central Banking," in *Money and Economy: Central Bankers' Views*, ed. by Pierluigi Ciocca (New York: St. Martin's Press).

Cagan, Phillip, 1984, *Report of the Gold Commission*, Carnegie-Rochester Conference Series on Public Policy, No. 20, pp. 247–73.

Cardoso, Eliana, 1991, "From Inertia to Megainflation: Brazil in the 1980s," in *Lessons of Economic Stabi-*

lization and Its Aftermath, ed. by Michael Bruno, Stanley Fischer, Elhanan Helpman, and Nissan Liviatan (Cambridge, Massachusetts: MIT Press).

Celâsun, Merih, and Dani Rodrik, 1987, "Debt Adjustment and Growth: Turkey," in *NBER Project on Developing Country Debt*, ed. by Jeffrey Sachs (Chicago: University of Chicago Press).

Central Bank of Iceland, 1993, *Annual Report 1992* (Reykjavik).

Chadha, Bankim, Paul Masson, and Guy Meredith, 1992, "Models of Inflation and the Costs of Disinflation," *Staff Papers*, International Monetary Fund, Vol. 39 (June), pp. 395–431.

Ciocca, Pierluigi, 1987, *Money and the Economy: Central Bankers' Views* (New York: St. Martin's Press).

Cline, William R., 1991, "Economic Stabilization in Peru," in *Lessons of Economic Stabilization and Its Aftermath*, ed. by Michael Bruno, Stanley Fischer, Elhanan Helpman, and Nissan Liviatan (Cambridge, Massachusetts: MIT Press).

Clower, Robert W., 1969, "Introduction," in *Monetary Theory*, ed. by R.W. Clower (London: Penguin).

Coats, W., 1994, "In Search of a Monetary Anchor: Commodity Standards Re-examined," in *Frameworks for Monetary Stability: Policy Issues and Country Experiences*, ed. by Tomás J.T. Baliño, T.J. and Carlo Cottarelli (Washington: International Monetary Fund).

Collyns, Charles, 1983, *Alternatives to the Central Bank in the Developing World*, IMF Occasional Paper No. 20 (Washington: International Monetary Fund).

Commission of Inquiry into the Monetary System and Monetary Policy in South Africa, 1978, *Exchange Rates in South Africa: Interim Report* (Pretoria: The Commission).

Committee to Review the Working of the Monetary System, 1985, *Report of the Committee to Review the Working of the Monetary System* (Bombay: Reserve Bank of India).

Cooper, Richard N., 1982, "The Gold Standard: Historical Facts and Future Prospects," *Brookings Paper on Economic Activity: 1* (Washington: Brookings Institution), pp. 1–56.

Cottarelli, Carlo, 1993, *Limiting Central Bank Credit to the Government: Theory and Practice*, IMF Occasional Paper No. 110 (Washington: International Monetary Fund).

Crazut, Rafael J., 1980, *El Banco Central de Venezuela: Notas sobre su historia y evolución—1940–1980* (Caracas: Banco Central de Venezuela).

Crockett, Andrew D., 1994, "Rules Versus Discretion in Monetary Policy," in *A Framework for Monetary Stability*, ed. by J.A.H. de Beaufort Wijnholds, S.C.W. Eijffinger, and L.H. Hoogduin (Dordrecht, Netherlands: Kluwer Academic Publishers).

Cukierman, Alex, 1992, *Central Bank Strategy, Credibility, and Independence: Theory and Evidence* (Cambridge, Massachusetts: MIT Press).

———, and A.H. Meltzer, 1986, "The Credibility of Monetary Announcements," in *Monetary Policy and Uncertainty*, ed. by Manfred J.M. Neumann (Baden-Baden: Nomos Verlagsgesellschaft).

Cukierman, Alex, Pedro Rodriguez, and Steven Webb, 1995, "Central Bank Autonomy and Exchange Rate Regimes—Their Effects on Monetary Accommodation and Activism," in *Positive Political Economy: Theory and Evidence,* ed. by Sylvester Eijffinger and Harry Huizinga (New York: John Wiley).

Dam, Kenneth W., 1982, *The Rules of the Game: Reform and Evolution in the International Monetary System* (Chicago: University of Chicago Press).

Davis, Kevin, and Mervyn Lewis, 1980, *Monetary Policy in Australia* (Melbourne: Longman Cheshire).

Davis, Richard G., 1977, "Monetary Objectives and Monetary Policy," *Quarterly Review* (New York: Federal Reserve Bank of New York, Spring).

De Beaufort Wijnholds, J.A.H., and G. Korteweg, 1991, "The Orientation of Monetary Policy and the Monetary Policy Decision-Making Process in the Netherlands," in *The Orientation of Monetary Policy and the Monetary Policy Decision-Making Process* (Basle: Bank for International Settlements).

De Grauwe, Paul, 1984, "Political Union and Monetary Union," in *Currency Competition and Monetary Union,* ed. by Pascal Salin (The Hague: Martinus Nijhoff Publishers).

——— , 1989, *The Cost of Disinflation and the European Monetary System,* Discussion Paper No. 326 (London: Centre for Economic Policy Research, July), pp. 1–33.

——— , and Victor Argy, 1990, *Choosing an Exchange Rate Regime: The Challenge for Smaller Industrial Countries* (Washington: International Monetary Fund).

——— , and Wim Vanhaverbeke, 1990, "Exchange Rate Experiences of Small EMS Countries: Belgium, Denmark, and the Netherlands," in *Choosing an Exchange Rate Regime: The Challenge for Smaller Industrial Countries,* ed. by Victor Argy and Paul De Grauwe (Washington: International Monetary Fund).

De Kock, M.H., 1974, *Central Banking* (London: Crosby Lockwood Staples, 4th ed.).

de Larosière, Jacques, 1994, "The Philosophy of Central Banking: A Panel Discussion," in *The Future of Central Banking,* ed. by Forrest Capie, Charles Goodhart, Stanley Fischer, and Norbert Schnadt (Cambridge, Massachusetts: Cambridge University Press).

Demsetz, H., 1967, "Toward a Theory of Property Rights," *American Economic Review,* Vol. 57, No. 2, pp. 347–59.

Diarrah, Cheick Oumar, 1990, *Mali: Bilan d'une gestion désastreuse* (Paris: L'Harmattan).

Dominguez, Kathryn M., 1993, "The Role of International Organizations in the Bretton Woods System," in *A Retrospective on the Bretton Woods System: Lessons for International Monetary Reform,* ed. by Michael D. Bordo and Barry Eichengreen (Chicago: University of Chicago Press).

Doré, Ansoumane, 1986, *Economie et société en République de Guinée, 1958–1984* (Chenove: Editions Bayardère).

Dornbusch, Rudiger, 1989, "Credibility, Debt, and Unemployment: Ireland's Failed Stabilization," *Economic Policy: A European Forum,* Vol. 4 (April), pp. 173–209.

Edey, M. L. and I. J. Macfarlane, 1991, "The Monetary Policy Decision-Making Process in Australia," in *The Orientation of Monetary Policy and the Monetary Policy Decision-Making Process* (Basle: Bank for International Settlements).

Edwards, Sebastian, 1995, "Exchange Rate Anchors and Inflation: A Political Economy Approach," in *Positive Political Economy: Theory and Evidence,* ed. by Sylvester Eijffinger and Harry Huizinga (New York: John Wiley).

——— , and Alejandra Cox Edwards, 1991, *Monetarism and Liberalization: The Chilean Experiment* (Chicago: University of Chicago Press).

Eggertsson, Thrainn, 1990, *Economic Behavior and Institutions* (Cambridge, Massachusetts: Cambridge University Press).

Eguidazu, Fernando, 1978, *Intervención monetaria y control de cambios en España (1900–1977)* (Madrid: Libros).

Eichengreen, B., 1991, *Monetary Regime Transformations* (Aldershot: Edward Elgar).

Eijffinger, S., and E. Schaling, 1993, "Central Bank Independence in Twelve Industrial Countries," *BNL Quarterly Review,* No. 184 (March).

Eijffinger, S., and M. Van Keulen, 1995, "Central Bank Independence in Another Eleven Countries," *BNL Quarterly Review,* No. 192 (March).

Elster, Jon, 1989, *The Cement of Society: A Study of Social Order* (Cambridge, Massachusetts: Cambridge University Press).

——— , 1994, "The Impact of Constitutions on Economic Performance," Proceedings of the World Bank's Annual Conference on Development Economics (Washington: World Bank).

Emerson, Michael, 1979, "The European Monetary System in the Broader Setting of the Community's Economic and Political Developments," in *The European Monetary System: Its Promise and Prospects*, ed. by Philip H. Trezise (Washington: Brookings Institution).

Ersel, Hasan, and Lerzan Iskenderoglu, 1993, "Monetary Programming in Turkey," in *Financial Liberalization in Turkey,* proceedings of a conference held in Washington, D.C., on December 28–30, 1990 (Ankara: Central Bank of the Republic of Turkey).

Escrivá, José Luis, and José Luis Malo de Molina, 1991, "Implementation of Spanish Monetary Policy in the Framework of European Integration," in *The Orientation of Monetary Policy and the Monetary Policy Decision-Making Process* (Basle: Bank for International Settlements).

Fama, E.F., 1980, "Banking in the Theory of Finance," *Journal of Monetary Economics,* Vol. 6 (January), pp. 39–57.

Fasano-Filho, Ugo, 1986, *Currency Substitution and Liberalization: The Case of Argentina* (Brookfield, Vermont: Gower Publishing Company).

Fazio, Antonio, 1996, "The Art of Central Banking," *Economic Bulletin*, Banca d'Italia, No. 23 (October), pp. 84–86.

Feldstein, Martin, 1993, "Lessons of the Bretton Woods Experience," in *A Retrospective on the Bretton Woods System: Lessons for International Monetary Reform,* ed. by Michael D. Bordo and Barry Eichengreen (Chicago: University of Chicago Press).

87

————— , 1992, "Europe's Monetary Union: The Case Against EMU," *The Economist* (June 13).

Fendt, Robert, Jr., 1981, "The Brazilian Experience with the Crawling Peg," in *Exchange Rate Rules: The Theory, Performance, and Prospects of the Crawling Peg*, ed. by John Williamson (New York: St. Martin's Press).

Fischer, Stanley, 1987, *Monetary Policy and Performance in the U.S., Japan, and Europe, 1973–86,* NBER Working Paper 2475 (Cambridge, Massachusetts: National Bureau of Economic Research).

————— , 1995a, "Central Bank Independence Revisited," *American Economic Review, Papers and Proceedings,* No. 85 (May), pp. 201–06.

————— , 1995b, *Modern Approaches to Central Banking,* NBER Working Paper 5064 (Cambridge, Massachusetts: National Bureau of Economic Research).

————— , 1996, "Why Are Central Banks Pursuing Long-Run Price Stability?" paper presented at the Federal Reserve Bank of Kansas City Symposium on Achieving Price Stability, Jackson Hole, Wyoming, August 29–31.

Flood, Robert P., and Peter Isard, 1989, "Monetary Policy Strategies," *Staff Papers,* International Monetary Fund, Vol. 36 (September), pp. 612–32.

Flood, Robert P., and Michael Mussa, 1994, *Issues Concerning Nominal Anchors for Monetary Policy* (Cambridge, Massachusetts: National Bureau of Economic Research).

Frankel, Jeffrey, and Menzie Chinn, 1995, "Stabilizing Properties of a Nominal GNP Rule," *Journal of Money, Credit and Banking*, Vol. 27 (May), pp. 318–34.

Friedman, Benjamin M., 1975, "Targets, Instruments, and Indicators of Monetary Policy," *Journal of Monetary Economics,* No. 1, pp. 443–73.

————— , 1982, *Time to Re-Examine the Monetary Targets Framework,* Discussion Paper Series 875 (Cambridge, Massachusetts: Harvard Institute of Economic Research), pp. 1–15.

————— , 1990, "Targets and Instruments of Monetary Policy," in *Handbook of Monetary Economics,* ed. by Benjamin M. Friedman and Frank H. Hahn, Volume II (Amsterdam: North Holland).

Friedman, Milton, 1961, "The Lag in Effect of Monetary Policy," *The Journal of Political Economy,* Vol. 69 (October), No. 5.

————— , 1984, "Monetary Policy for the 1980s," in *To Promote Prosperity: U.S. Domestic Policy in the Mid-1980s,* ed. by John H. Moore (Stanford: Hoover Institution Press).

Fry, Maxwell J., Charles A. E. Goodhart, and Alvaro Almeida, 1995, "Central Banking in Developing Countries: Objectives, Activities, and Independence," paper presented at the Symposium on Central Banking in Developing Countries, Bank of England, London, June 9.

Gayle, Dennis John, 1986, *The Small Developing State: Comparing Political Economies in Costa Rica, Singapore and Jamaica* (Brookfield, Vermont: Gower Publishing Company).

Ghosh, Atish R., Anne-Marie Gulde, Jonathan D. Ostry, and Holger C. Wolf, 1995, "Does the Nominal Exchange Rate Regime Matter?" IMF Working Paper No. 95/121 (Washington: International Monetary Fund).

Giannini, Curzio, 1994, "Confidence Costs and the Institutional Genesis of Central Banks," *Temi di Discussione,* No. 226 (Rome: Banca d'Italia), pp. 1–77.

————— , 1995, "Money, Trust and Central Banking," *Journal of Economics and Business,* Vol. 47, No. 2 (May), pp. 217–37.

Giavazzi, Francesco, and Alberto Giovannini, 1986, "EMS and the Dollar," *Economic Policy: A European Forum,* Vol. 1 (April), pp. 455–84.

————— , and Alberto Giovannini, 1989, *Limiting Exchange Rate Flexibility: The European Monetary System* (Cambridge, Massachusetts: MIT Press).

Giorgi, Eduardo, 1991, *Inflation under Different External Regimes: The Case of Uruguay* (Aldershot: Avebury).

Giovannini, Alberto, 1989, "How Do Fixed-Exchange-Rate Regimes Work? Evidence from the Gold Standard, Bretton Woods and the EMS," in *Blueprints for Exchange-Rate Management,* ed. by Marcus Miller, Barry Eichengreen, and Richards Portes (London: Academic Press).

————— , 1993, "Bretton Woods and Its Precursors: Rules versus Discretion in the History of International Monetary Regimes," in *A Retrospective on the Bretton Woods System: Lessons for International Monetary Reform,* ed. by Michael D. Bordo and Barry Eichengreen (Chicago: University of Chicago Press).

Goedhart, C., 1985, "Zijlstra's Concerto Grosso," in *Jelle Zijlstra, A Central Banker's View: Selected Speeches and Articles*, ed. by C. Goedhart, G.A. Kessler, J. Kymmell, and F. De Roos (Dordrecht, Netherlands: Martinus Nijhoff Publishers).

Gold, Joseph, 1979, *Conditionality,* IMF Pamphlet Series, No. 31 (Washington: International Monetary Fund).

Goodfriend, Marvin, 1994, *Acquiring and Maintaining Credibility for Low Inflation: The U.S. Experience,* paper presented at the CEPR Workshop on Inflation Targets, Milan, November 25–26.

Goodman, John B., 1992, *Monetary Sovereignty: The Politics of Central Banking in Western Europe* (Ithaca: Cornell University Press).

Greenfield, Robert L., and Leland B. Yeager, 1983, "A Laissez-Faire Approach to Monetary Stability," *Journal of Money, Credit and Banking*, No. 3 (August), pp. 302–15.

Greenspan, Alan, 1993, "Statement to the Congress," *Federal Reserve Bulletin Board of Governors of the Federal Reserve System,* Vol. 79 (September), pp. 849–55.

Griffiths, Brian, and Geoffrey E. Wood, eds., 1981a, *Monetary Targets* (New York: St. Martin's Press).

————— , "Introduction," 1981, in *Monetary Targets,* ed. by Brian Griffiths and Geoffrey E. Wood (New York: St. Martin's Press).

Grilli, Vittorio, and Gian Maria Milesi-Ferretti, 1995, *Economic Effects and Structural Determinants of Capital Controls,* Working Paper 95/31 (Washington: International Monetary Fund).

Gros, Daniel, 1988, "Discussion," in *The European Monetary System,* ed. by Francesco Giavazzi, Stefano Micossi, and Marcus Miller (Cambridge, Massachusetts: Cambridge University Press).

Guardia Quirós, Jorge, 1993, *Del cambio fijo a la liberalización cambiaria: colección de ensayos* (San José, Costa Rica: Litografía e Imprenta Lil).

Guisinger, Stephen E., 1981, "Stabilization Policies in Pakistan: The 1970–77 Experience," in *Economic Stabilization in Developing Countries,* ed. by William R. Cline and Sidney Weintraub (Washington: Brookings Institution).

Guitián, Manuel, 1992, *The Unique Nature of the Responsibilities of the International Monetary Fund,* IMF Pamphlet Series, No. 31 (Washington: International Monetary Fund).

——— , 1994a, "The Role of Monetary Policy in IMF Programs," in *A Framework for Monetary Stability,* ed. by J.A.H. de Beaufort Wijnholds, S.C.W. Eijffinger, and L.H. Hoogduin (Dordrecht, Netherlands: Kluwer Academic Publishers).

——— , 1994b, "Rules or Discretion in Monetary Policy: National and International Perspectives," in *Frameworks for Monetary Stability: Policy Issues and Country Experiences,* ed. by Tomás J. T. Baliño and Carlo Cottarelli (Washington: International Monetary Fund).

——— , 1995, "Conditionality: Past, Present, Future," *Staff Papers,* International Monetary Fund, Vol. 42 (December), pp. 792–835.

Gylfason, Thorvaldur, 1990, "Exchange Rate Policy, Inflation, and Unemployment: The Nordic EFTA Countries," in *Choosing an Exchange Rate Regime: The Challenge for Smaller Industrial Countries,* ed. by Victor Argy and Paul De Grauwe (Washington: International Monetary Fund).

Hadjimichael, Michael T., Thomas Rumbaugh, and Eric Verreydt, 1992, *The Gambia: Economic Adjustment in a Small Open Economy,* IMF Occasional Paper No. 100 (Washington: International Monetary Fund).

Hall, Robert E., 1983, "Optimal Fiduciary Monetary Systems," *Journal of Monetary Economics,* Vol. 1 (July), pp. 33–54.

Hamann, A. Javier, and Carlos E. Paredes, 1991, "The Peruvian Economy: Characteristics and Trends," in *Peru's Path to Recovery: A Plan for Economic Stabilization and Growth,* ed. by Carlos E. Paredes and Jeffrey Sachs (Washington: Brookings Institution).

Hansen, Bent, 1991, *World Bank Comparative Studies. Political Economy of Poverty, Equity, and Growth—Egypt and Turkey* (Oxford: Oxford University Press).

Hayek, F. A. von, 1978, *Denationalization of Money: The Argument Refined: An Analysis of the Theory and Practice of Concurrent Currencies,* 2nd ed. (London: Institute of Economic Affairs).

Hazlewood, Arthur, 1979, *The Economy of Kenya: The Kenyatta Era* (Oxford: Oxford University Press).

Helpman, Elhanan, Leonardo Leiderman, and Gil Bufman, 1994, "New Breed of Exchange Rate Bands: Chile, Israel and Mexico," *Economic Policy: A European Forum,* Vol. 9 (October), pp. 260–306.

Heymann, Daniel, 1991, "From Sharp Disinflation to Hyperinflation, Twice: The Argentine Experience, 1985–1989," in *Lessons of Economic Stabilization and Its Aftermath,* ed. by Michael Bruno, Stanley Fischer, Elhanan Helpman, and Nissan Liviatan (Cambridge, Massachusetts: MIT Press).

Hicks, John R., 1989, *A Market Theory of Money* (Oxford: Clarendon Press).

Hochreiter, Eduard, and Helmut Pech, 1991, "The Orientation of Monetary Policy and the Monetary Policy Decision-Making Process: The Austrian Case," in *The Orientation of Monetary Policy and the Monetary Policy Decision-Making Process* (Basle: Bank for International Settlement).

Hochreiter, Eduard, and Åke Tornquist, 1990, "Austria's Monetary and Exchange Rate Policy: Some Comparative Remarks with Respect to Sweden," *De Pecunia,* Vol. II, No. 2–3 (October).

Hock Pang, Khaw, and Ng Goo Phai, 1983, "Fiscal and Monetary Management in Malaysia: Some Points for Consideration," *UMBC Economic Review,* Vol. 19, No.1, pp. 29–39.

Holden, Merle, and Paul Holden, 1981, "Policy Objectives, Country Characteristics, and the Choice of Exchange Rate Regime," *Rivista Internazionale di Scienze Economiche e Commerciali,* Vol. 28 (October–November), pp. 1001–14.

Icard, André, 1994, "Monetary Policy and Exchange Rates: The French Experience," in *Framework for Monetary Stability,* ed. by J.A.H. de Beaufort Wijnholds, S.C.W. Eijffinger, and L.H. Hoogduin (Dordrecht, Netherlands: Kluwer Academic Publishers).

Irfan-ul-Haque, 1987, *A Compendium of Pakistan Economy* (Karachi: Royal Book Company).

Isard, Peter, and Liliana Rojas-Suarez, 1986, "Velocity of Money and the Practice of Monetary Targeting: Experience, Theory, and the Policy Debate," *Staff Studies for the World Economic Outlook* (Washington: International Monetary Fund).

Issing, Otmar, 1995, "Is Monetary Targeting in Germany Still Adequate?" *Auszüge aus Presseartikeln,* No. 46 (June) (Frankfurt: Deutsche Bundesbank), pp. 5–10.

Johnson, David R., and Pierre L. Siklos, 1992, "Empirical Evidence on the Independence of Central Banks" (mimeo: Wilford Laurier University).

Joseph, Mathew, 1992, *Exchange Rate Policy: Impact on Exports and Balance of Payments* (New Delhi: Deep & Deep Publications).

Kapur, Ishan, Michael T. Hadjimichael, Paul Hilbers, Jerald Schiff, and Philippe Szymczak, 1991, *Ghana: Adjustment and Growth, 1983–91,* IMF Occasional Paper No. 86 (Washington: International Monetary Fund).

Khan, Aftab Ahmad, 1993, "The Right Approach to Monetary Policies," *Pakistan and Gulf Economist,* No. 12 (May), pp. 14–16.

Kiguel, Miguel A., and Nissan Liviatan, 1994, "Exchange-Rate-Based Stabilizations in Argentina and Chile: A Fresh Outlook," in *Frameworks for Monetary Stability: Policy Issues and Country Experiences,* ed. by Tomás J. T. Baliño and Carlo Cottarelli (Washington: International Monetary Fund).

Kopits, George, 1987, *Structural Reform, Stabilization, and Growth in Turkey,* IMF Occasional Paper No. 52 (Washington: International Monetary Fund).

Krugman, Paul, 1995, "Dutch Tulips and Emerging Markets," *Foreign Affairs,* No. 74 (July–August), pp. 28–44.

Kydland, F. E., and C. Prescott, 1977, "Rules Rather than Discretion: The Inconsistency of Optimal Plans," *Journal of Political Economy*, No. 85, pp. 473–92.

Lambert, Marie-Henriette, and Eric Jacobs, 1991, "The Monetary Policy Decision-Making Process in Belgium," *The Orientation of Monetary Policy and the Monetary Policy Decision-Making Process* (Basle: Bank for International Settlements).

Larrain, Felipe, and Jeffrey D. Sachs, 1991, "Exchange Rate and Monetary Policy," in *Peru's Path to Recovery: A Plan for Economic Stabilization and Growth,* ed. by Carlos E. Paredes and Jeffrey Sachs (Washington: Brookings Institution).

Lindberg, Leon N., and Charles S. Maier, eds., 1985, *The Politics of Inflation and Economic Stagnation: Theoretical Approaches and International Case Studies* (Washington: Brookings Institution).

Lindgren, Carl-Johan, and Daniel Dueñas, 1994, "Strengthening Central Bank Independence in Latin America," in *Frameworks for Monetary Stability: Policy Issues and Country Experiences*, ed. by Tomás J.T. Baliño and Carlo Cottarelli (Washington: International Monetary Fund).

Liviatan, Nissan, ed., 1993, *Proceedings of a Conference on Currency Substitution and Currency Boards* (Washington: World Bank).

Llewellyn, David, 1982, "Monetary Targets," in *The Framework of U.K. Monetary Policy,* ed. by David Llewellyn, G.E.J. Dennis, Maximilian J.B. Hall, and J.G. Nellis (London: Heinemann Educational Books).

Lohmann, Susanne, 1992, "Optimal Commitment in Monetary Policy: Credibility Versus Flexibility," *American Economic Review*, Vol. 82 (March), pp. 273–86.

Lundahl, Mats, and Lennart Petersson, 1991, *The Dependent Economy: Lesotho and the Southern African Customs Union* (Boulder: Westview Press).

Madigan, Brian F., 1994, "The Design of U.S. Monetary Policy: Targets, Indicators, and Information Variables," in *Frameworks for Monetary Stability: Policy Issues and Country Experiences*, ed. by Tomás J. T. Baliño and Carlo Cottarelli (Washington: International Monetary Fund).

Marston, Richard C., 1987, *Exchange Rate Policy Reconsidered,* NBER Working Paper 2310 (Cambridge, Massachusetts: National Bureau of Economic Research).

Mas, Ignacio, 1995, "Central Bank Independence: A Critical View From a Developing Country Perspective," *World Development,* Vol. 23 (October), pp. 1639–52.

McCallum, B. T., 1995, "Two Fallacies Concerning Central Bank Independence," *American Economic Review, Papers and Proceedings,* Vol. 85 (May), pp. 207–11.

———, 1996, "Crucial Issues Concerning Central Bank Independence," NBER Working Paper 5597 (Cambridge, Massachusetts: National Bureau of Economic Research).

Mecagni, Mauro, and Susan M. Schadler, 1995, "The Experience with Nominal Anchors," *IMF Conditionality: Experience Under Stand-By and Extended Arrangements—Part II—Background Papers,* IMF Occasional Paper No. 129 (Washington: International Monetary Fund).

Melton, William C., and V. Vance Roley, 1990, "Federal Reserve Behavior Since 1980: A Financial Markets Perspective," in *The Political Economy of American Monetary Policy*, ed. by Thomas Mayer (Cambridge, Massachusetts: Cambridge University Press).

Nordhaus, W. D., 1990, "The Political Business Cycle," *Review of Economic Studies,* No. 42, pp. 169–70.

Norges Bank, 1994, "Norway's Monetary and Exchange Rate Policy Under a Floating Exchange Rate Regime," *Economic Paper,* No. 65 (June), pp. 136–47.

North, Douglas C., 1990, *Institutions, Institutional Change and Economic Performance* (Cambridge, Massachusetts: Cambridge University Press).

Nsouli, Saleh M., Sena Eken, Klaus Enders, Van-Can Thai, Jörg Decressin, and Filippo Cartiglia, 1995, *Resilience and Growth Through Sustained Adjustment: The Moroccan Experience,* IMF Occasional Paper No. 117 (Washington: International Monetary Fund).

O'Grady Walshe, T., 1991, "Managing a Central Bank: Goals, Strategies, and Techniques," in *The Evolving Role of Central Banks*, ed. by Patrick Downes and Reza Vaez-Zadeh (Washington: International Monetary Fund).

Ojeda, Galo Abril, 1985, *Política monetaria y desarrollo industrial en el Ecuador (1970–1983)* (Quito: Banco Central del Ecuador).

Okongwu, Chu S. P., 1986, *The Nigerian Economy: Being an Anatomy of a Traumatized Economy with Some Proposals for Stabilization* (Enugu, Nigeria: Fourth Dimension Publishing Company).

Onoh, J.K., 1980, *The Foundations of Nigeria's Financial Infrastructure* (London: Croom Helm).

Organization for Economic Cooperation and Development, 1990, *OECD Economic Surveys: Iceland* (Paris: OECD).

Ortiz, Guillermo, 1991, "Mexico Beyond the Debt Crisis: Toward Sustainable Growth with Price Stability," in *Lessons of Economic Stabilization and Its Aftermath,* ed. by Michael Bruno, Stanley Fischer, Elhanan Helpman, and Nissan Liviatan (Cambridge, Massachusetts: MIT Press).

Paleologos, John M., 1993, "Investigation on the Effectiveness of the Devaluation Policy in the Case of the Greek Economy: 1975 (I)–1991 (I)," *Economia Internazionale,* Vol. 46 (May–August), pp. 247–58.

Pascale, Ricardo, 1990, *Conferencias sobre política económica, 1985–1990* (Montevideo: Banco Central del Uruguay).

Passacantando, Franco, 1995, "Monetary Reforms and Monetary Policy in Italy 1979–94," paper presented at the conference on The Quest for Monetary Stability, held by the Getúlio Vargas Foundation, Rio de Janeiro.

Perez, Lorenzo, L., 1994, "Case Study of Venezuela," in *Approaches to Exchange Rate Policy,* ed. by Richard C. Barth and Chorng-Huey Wong (Washington: International Monetary Fund).

Persson, Torsten, and Guido Tabellini, 1993, "Designing Institutions for Monetary Stability," *Carnegie Rochester Conference Series on Public Policy,* No. 39 (December), pp. 53–94.

———, 1994, "Introduction," in *Monetary and Fiscal Policy—Volume 1: Credibility,* ed. by Torsten Persson and Guido Tabellini (Cambridge, Massachusetts: MIT Press).

Pollard, S. Patricia, 1993, "Central Bank Independence and Economic Performance," *Federal Reserve Bank of St. Louis, Quarterly Review*, No. 75 (July/August), pp. 21–36.

Posen, Adam S., 1993, "Why Central Bank Independence Does Not Cause Low Inflation: There Is No Institutional Fix for Politics," in *Finance and the International Economy,* ed. by R. O'Brien (Oxford: Oxford University Press).

Proske, Dieter, and Walter Penker, 1995, "Central Bank Research as a Competitive Element in an Economic and Monetary Union," *Economic and Financial Modelling* (Winter), pp. 165–87.

Quirk, Peter J., 1994, "Fixed or Floating Exchange Regimes: Does It Matter for Inflation?" IMF Working Paper No. 94/134 (Washington: International Monetary Fund).

Ramos, Joseph, 1986, *Neoconservative Economics in the Southern Cone of Latin America, 1973–1983* (Baltimore: Johns Hopkins University Press).

Rangarajan, C., 1987, "Analytical Framework of the Chakravarty Committee Report on the Monetary System," *Reserve Bank of India Bulletin*, No. 41 (September), pp. 702–05.

———, 1988, "Issues in Monetary Management," *Reserve Bank of India Bulletin*, No. 42 (December), pp. 1104–13.

Reejal, Pushkar R., 1986, *Monetary and Credit Policies of the Nepal Rastra Bank and Their Impact on the Nepalese Economy* (Kathmandu: Ratna Pustak Bhandar).

Reserve Bank of New Zealand, 1979, *Annual Report for 1978.*

———, 1994, *Monetary Policy and the New Zealand Financial System* (Reserve Bank of New Zealand: Hutcheson Bowman and Stewart).

Rich, G., 1991, "The Orientation of Monetary Policy and the Monetary Policy Decision-Making Process in Switzerland," in *The Orientation of Monetary Policy and the Monetary Policy Decision-Making Process* (Basle: Bank for International Settlements).

Rogoff, Kenneth, 1985, "The Optimal Degree of Commitment to an Intermediate Monetary Target," *Quarterly Journal of Economics*, No. 100 (November), pp. 1169–90.

———, 1985b, "Can Exchange Rate Predictability Be Achieved Without Monetary Convergence? Evidence from the EMS," *European Economic Review*, No. 28 (June/July), pp. 93–115.

Sachs, Jeffrey, 1986, "Bolivian Hyperinflation and Stabilization," NBER Working Paper 2073 (Cambridge, Massachusetts: National Bureau of Economic Research).

Sarcinelli, Mario, 1989, "The European Monetary System Ten Years After Its Creation," *The European Monetary System Ten Years After Its Creation: Results and Prospects* (Rome: Instituto Mobiliare Italiano).

Sawamoto, Kuniho, and Nobuyuki Ichikawa, 1994, "Implementation of Monetary Policy in Japan," in *Frameworks for Monetary Stability: Policy Issues and Country Experiences*, ed. by Tomás J. T. Baliño and Carlo Cottarelli (Washington: International Monetary Fund).

Schadler, Susan M., and others, 1995, *IMF Conditionality: Experience Under Stand-By and Extended Arrangements—Part I—Key Issues and Findings,* IMF Occasional Paper No. 129 (Washington: International Monetary Fund).

Schelling, T., 1982, "Establishing Credibility: Strategic Considerations," *American Economic Review, Papers and Proceedings* (May), pp. 77–80.

Schiltknecht, Kurt, 1981, "Targeting the Base—The Swiss Experience," in *Monetary Targets*, ed. by Brian Griffiths and Geoffrey E. Wood (New York: St. Martin's Press).

Schmitt, Hans O., 1981, *Economic Stabilization and Growth in Portugal*, Occasional Paper No. 2 (Washington: International Monetary Fund).

See Yan, Lin, 1991, "Interaction of Exchange Rate Policy and Monetary Policy: The Case of Malaysia," in *Monetary Policy Instruments for Developing Countries,* ed. by Gerard Caprio, Jr. and Patrick Honohan (Washington: World Bank).

Selgin, George, 1994, "On Ensuring the Acceptability of a New Fiat Money," *Journal of Money, Credit and Banking*, Vol. 26 (November), pp. 808–26.

Sharer, Robert L., Hema R. De Zoysa, and Calvin A. McDonald, 1995, *Uganda: Adjustment with Growth, 1987–94,* IMF Occasional Paper No. 121 (Washington: International Monetary Fund).

Sharma, Gunanidhi, 1987, *Monetary Structure of the Nepalese Economy: Policy Issues in Theory and Practice* (New Delhi: South Asian Publishers).

Smith, Michael R., 1992, *Power, Norms and Inflation: A Skeptical Treatment* (New York: Aldine de Gruyter).

South African Reserve Bank, 1986, *Annual Report on 1985* (Pretoria).

Stiehler, Ulrich, 1995, "The New Monetary Policy Framework of the United Kingdom," IMF Paper on Policy Analysis and Assessment, 95/1 (Washington: International Monetary Fund).

Stockman, Alan C., 1988, "Real Exchange Rate Variability Under Pegged and Floating Nominal Exchange Rate Systems: An Equilibrium Theory," NBER Working Paper 2565 (Cambridge, Massachusetts: National Bureau of Economic Research).

Svensson, Lars E.O., 1995, "The Swedish Experience of an Inflation Target," in *Inflation Targets*, ed. by Leonardo Leiderman and Lars E.O. Svensson (London: Centre for Economic Policy Research).

———, 1994, "Fixed Exchange Rates as a Means to Price Stability: What Have We Learned?" *European Economic Review* No. 38 (April), pp. 447–68.

Taylor, John B., 1985, "What Would Nominal GNP Targeting Do to the Business Cycle?" *Carnegie-Rochester Conference Series on Public Policies*, No. 22, pp. 61–84.

Tschinkel, Sheila, and John S. Hill, 1976, "The Strategy of Monetary Control," *Monthly Review* (New York: Federal Reserve Bank of New York).

Townend, John C., 1991, "The Orientation of Monetary Policy and the Monetary Policy Decision-Making Process in the United Kingdom," *The Orientation of Monetary Policy and the Monetary Policy Decision-Making Process* (Basle: Bank for International Settlements).

Urrutia, Miguel, 1981, "Experience with the Crawling Peg in Colombia," in *Exchange Rate Rules: The Theory, Performance, and Prospects of the Crawling Peg*, ed. by John Williamson (New York: St. Martin's Press).

van Ypersele, Jacques, and Jean-Claude Koeune, 1984, "The European Monetary System: Origins, Operation and Outlook" (Luxembourg: Commission of the European Communities).

Végh, Carlos A., 1992, "Stopping High Inflation: An Analytical Overview," *Staff Papers*, International Monetary Fund, Vol. 39 (September), pp. 626–95.

Volcker, Paul, and Toyoo Gyothen, 1992, *Changing Fortunes: The World's Money and the Threat to American Leadership* (New York: Times Books).

Walsh, Carl E., 1995, "Optimal Contracts for Central Bankers," *American Economic Review*, Vol. 85 (March), pp. 150–67.

Weintraub, Sidney, 1981, "Case Study of Economic Stabilization: Mexico," in *Economic Stabilization in Developing Countries*, ed. by William R. Cline and Sidney Weintraub (Washington: Brookings Institution).

Williamson, John, ed., 1981, *Exchange Rate Rules: The Theory, Performance, and Prospects of the Crawling Peg* (New York: St. Martin's Press).

Wood, John H., 1992, "Monetary Policy in a Small Open Economy: The Case of Singapore," *Economic Review*, No. 2 (Dallas: Federal Reserve Bank), pp. 25–41.

World Bank, 1980, *Zaïre: Current Economic Situation and Constraints* (Washington: World Bank).

———, 1992, *Paraguay: Country Economic Memorandum* (Washington: World Bank).

Yeager, Leland B., ed., 1962, *In Search of a Monetary Constitution* (Cambridge, Massachusetts: Harvard University Press).

Zolotas, Xenophon, 1978, *Inflation and the Monetary Target in Greece: An Address,* Papers and Lectures, No. 38 (Athens: Bank of Greece).

Recent Occasional Papers of the International Monetary Fund

154. Credibility Without Rules? Monetary Frameworks in the Post–Bretton Woods Era, by Carlo Cottarelli and Curzio Giannini. 1997.

153. Pension Regimes and Saving, by G.A. Mackenzie, Philip Gerson, and Alfredo Cuevas. 1997.

152. Hong Kong, China: Growth, Structural Change, and Economic Stability During the Transition, by John Dodsworth and Dubravko Mihaljek. 1997.

151. Currency Board Arrangements: Issues and Experiences, by a staff team led by Tomás J.T. Baliño and Charles Enoch. 1997.

150. Kuwait: From Reconstruction to Accumulation for Future Generations, by Nigel Andrew Chalk, Mohamed A. El-Erian, Susan J. Fennell, Alexei P. Kireyev, and John F. Wison. 1997.

149. The Composition of Fiscal Adjustment and Growth: Lessons from Fiscal Reforms in Eight Economies, by G.A. Mackenzie, David W.H. Orsmond, and Philip R. Gerson. 1997.

148. Nigeria: Experience with Structural Adjustment, by Gary Moser, Scott Rogers, and Reinold van Til, with Robin Kibuka and Inutu Lukonga. 1997.

147. Aging Populations and Public Pension Schemes, by Sheetal K. Chand and Albert Jaeger. 1996

146. Thailand: The Road to Sustained Growth, by Kalpana Kochhar, Louis Dicks-Mireaux, Balazs Horvath, Mauro Mecagni, Erik Offerdal, and Jianping Zhou. 1996.

145. Exchange Rate Movements and Their Impact on Trade and Investment in the APEC Region, by Takatoshi Ito, Peter Isard, Steven Symansky, and Tamim Bayoumi. 1996.

144. National Bank of Poland: The Road to Indirect Instruments, by Piero Ugolini. 1996.

143. Adjustment for Growth: The African Experience, by Michael T. Hadjimichael, Michael Nowak, Robert Sharer, and Amor Tahari. 1996.

142. Quasi-Fiscal Operations of Public Financial Institutions, by G.A. Mackenzie and Peter Stella. 1996.

141. Monetary and Exchange System Reforms in China: An Experiment in Gradualism, by Hassanali Mehran, Marc Quintyn, Tom Nordman, and Bernard Laurens. 1996.

140. Government Reform in New Zealand, by Graham C. Scott. 1996.

139. Reinvigorating Growth in Developing Countries: Lessons from Adjustment Policies in Eight Economies, by David Goldsbrough, Sharmini Coorey, Louis Dicks-Mireaux, Balazs Horvath, Kalpana Kochhar, Mauro Mecagni, Erik Offerdal, and Jianping Zhou. 1996.

138. Aftermath of the CFA Franc Devaluation, by Jean A.P. Clément, with Johannes Mueller, Stéphane Cossé, and Jean Le Dem. 1996.

137. The Lao People's Democratic Republic: Systemic Transformation and Adjustment, edited by Ichiro Otani and Chi Do Pham. 1996.

136. Jordan: Strategy for Adjustment and Growth, edited by Edouard Maciejewski and Ahsan Mansur. 1996.

135. Vietnam: Transition to a Market Economy, by John R. Dodsworth, Erich Spitäller, Michael Braulke, Keon Hyok Lee, Kenneth Miranda, Christian Mulder, Hisanobu Shishido, and Krishna Srinivasan. 1996.

134. India: Economic Reform and Growth, by Ajai Chopra, Charles Collyns, Richard Hemming, and Karen Parker with Woosik Chu and Oliver Fratzscher. 1995.

133. Policy Experiences and Issues in the Baltics, Russia, and Other Countries of the Former Soviet Union, edited by Daniel A. Citrin and Ashok K. Lahiri. 1995.

132. Financial Fragilities in Latin America: The 1980s and 1990s, by Liliana Rojas-Suárez and Steven R. Weisbrod. 1995.

131. Capital Account Convertibility: Review of Experience and Implications for IMF Policies, by staff teams headed by Peter J. Quirk and Owen Evans. 1995.

130. Challenges to the Swedish Welfare State, by Desmond Lachman, Adam Bennett, John H. Green, Robert Hagemann, and Ramana Ramaswamy. 1995.

129. IMF Conditionality: Experience Under Stand-By and Extended Arrangements. Part II: Background Papers. Susan Schadler, Editor, with Adam Bennett, Maria Carkovic, Louis Dicks-Mireaux, Mauro Mecagni, James H.J. Morsink, and Miguel A. Savastano. 1995.

128. IMF Conditionality: Experience Under Stand-By and Extended Arrangements. Part I: Key Issues and Findings, by Susan Schadler, Adam Bennett, Maria Carkovic, Louis Dicks-Mireaux, Mauro Mecagni, James H.J. Morsink, and Miguel A. Savastano. 1995.

127. Road Maps of the Transition: The Baltics, the Czech Republic, Hungary, and Russia, by Biswajit Banerjee, Vincent Koen, Thomas Krueger, Mark S. Lutz, Michael Marrese, and Tapio O. Saavalainen. 1995.

126. The Adoption of Indirect Instruments of Monetary Policy, by a staff team headed by William E. Alexander, Tomás J.T. Baliño, and Charles Enoch. 1995.

125. United Germany: The First Five Years—Performance and Policy Issues, by Robert Corker, Robert A. Feldman, Karl Habermeier, Hari Vittas, and Tessa van der Willigen. 1995.

124. Saving Behavior and the Asset Price "Bubble" in Japan: Analytical Studies, edited by Ulrich Baumgartner and Guy Meredith. 1995.

123. Comprehensive Tax Reform: The Colombian Experience, edited by Parthasarathi Shome. 1995.

122. Capital Flows in the APEC Region, edited by Mohsin S. Khan and Carmen M. Reinhart. 1995.

121. Uganda: Adjustment with Growth, 1987–94, by Robert L. Sharer, Hema R. De Zoysa, and Calvin A. McDonald. 1995.

120. Economic Dislocation and Recovery in Lebanon, by Sena Eken, Paul Cashin, S. Nuri Erbas, Jose Martelino, and Adnan Mazarei. 1995.

119. Singapore: A Case Study in Rapid Development, edited by Kenneth Bercuson with a staff team comprising Robert G. Carling, Aasim M. Husain, Thomas Rumbaugh, and Rachel van Elkan. 1995.

118. Sub-Saharan Africa: Growth, Savings, and Investment, by Michael T. Hadjimichael, Dhaneshwar Ghura, Martin Mühleisen, Roger Nord, and E. Murat Uçer. 1995.

117. Resilience and Growth Through Sustained Adjustment: The Moroccan Experience, by Saleh M. Nsouli, Sena Eken, Klaus Enders, Van-Can Thai, Jörg Decressin, and Filippo Cartiglia, with Janet Bungay. 1995.

116. Improving the International Monetary System: Constraints and Possibilities, by Michael Mussa, Morris Goldstein, Peter B. Clark, Donald J. Mathieson, and Tamim Bayoumi. 1994.

115. Exchange Rates and Economic Fundamentals: A Framework for Analysis, by Peter B. Clark, Leonardo Bartolini, Tamim Bayoumi, and Steven Symansky. 1994.

114. Economic Reform in China: A New Phase, by Wanda Tseng, Hoe Ee Khor, Kalpana Kochhar, Dubravko Mihaljek, and David Burton. 1994.

113. Poland: The Path to a Market Economy, by Liam P. Ebrill, Ajai Chopra, Charalambos Christofides, Paul Mylonas, Inci Otker, and Gerd Schwartz. 1994.

112. The Behavior of Non-Oil Commodity Prices, by Eduardo Borensztein, Mohsin S. Khan, Carmen M. Reinhart, and Peter Wickham. 1994.

111. The Russian Federation in Transition: External Developments, by Benedicte Vibe Christensen. 1994.

110. Limiting Central Bank Credit to the Government: Theory and Practice, by Carlo Cottarelli. 1993.

109. The Path to Convertibility and Growth: The Tunisian Experience, by Saleh M. Nsouli, Sena Eken, Paul Duran, Gerwin Bell, and Zühtü Yücelik. 1993.

108. Recent Experiences with Surges in Capital Inflows, by Susan Schadler, Maria Carkovic, Adam Bennett, and Robert Kahn. 1993.

107. China at the Threshold of a Market Economy, by Michael W. Bell, Hoe Ee Khor, and Kalpana Kochhar with Jun Ma, Simon N'guiamba, and Rajiv Lall. 1993.

Note: For information on the title and availability of Occasional Papers not listed, please consult the IMF Publications Catalog or contact IMF Publication Services.